Molecules in the air

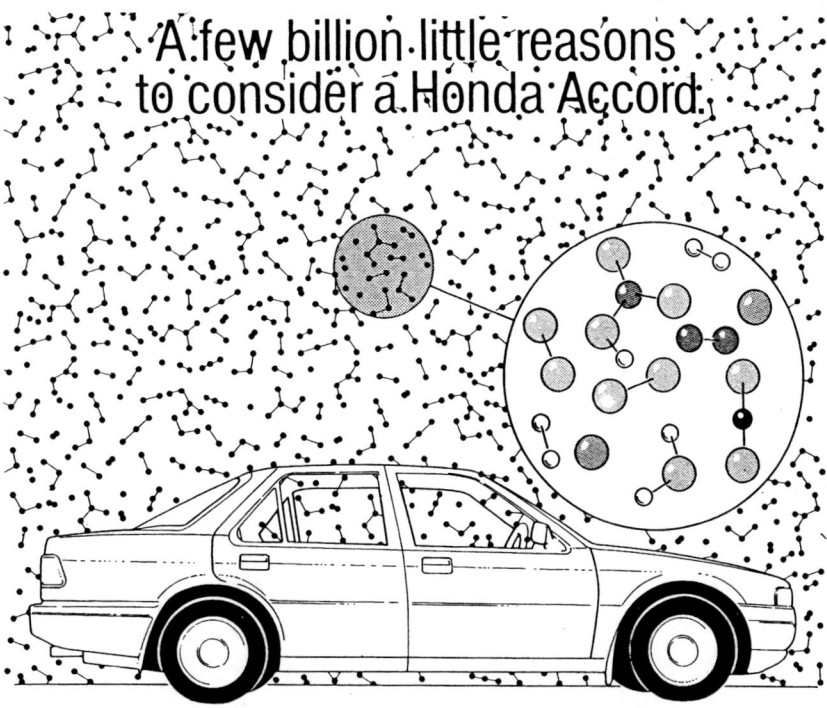

You don't drive a car in a vacuum. It, and you, are surrounded. By nitrogen, by oxygen, by argon, by rare compounds with strange names. In short, by that molecular soup we call air.

If that sounds like a statement of the obvious, then what follows is not. Air affects the performance of car and driver in a host of unexpected ways. Oxygen plays a vital role in the engine. Airborne corrosive agents like nitric acid can play havoc with your paintwork.

This is part of an advertisement for Honda cars. (The advertisement has been slightly modified, because the original was in colour). The advertiser is trying to show that air is a complicated mixture of elements and compounds, of atoms and molecules, which can affect cars in many ways.

An *element* cannot be split into anything simpler. It is made up of just one sort of atom,

For example or

Sometimes, these atoms may go around by themselves,

but more commonly they join together in pairs,

Two or more atoms joined together are called *molecules*. A *compound* is composed of two or more different sorts of atoms joined together to form molecules.

For example,  or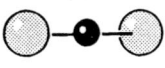

turn

© Borrows, Foster and Richardson 1991

1 a The advertisement says we don't drive cars *in a vacuum*. What do we drive cars in?
  b Give *one* reason why cars would not work in a vacuum.

2 The advertisement mentions the *names* of four chemicals. One of these is nitric acid. Find the others, and then copy and complete this table:

Name of chemical	Is it an element or a compound?
Nitric acid	

3 a Explain why the advertisement talks about "A few <u>billion</u> <u>little</u> reasons". Be sure to comment on both of the underlined words.
  b In what way(s) is the drawing *not* a realistic representation of molecules in the air?

4 a You probably know the names of the main gases present in air. What are they? What percentage of each is there in normal air?
  b Air is one example of a mixture that occurs naturally. Give *two* more examples.

5 There are seven different chemicals (1, 2, ... 7) represented in the drawings in the advertisement. These are shown in the first two columns of the table below.
Copy the table carefully, and complete it.

6 It would be rather boring having to do these drawings all the time, so chemists often use a sort of shorthand. A chemical symbol consists of one or two letters. These are the symbols for the atoms shown in the advertisement:

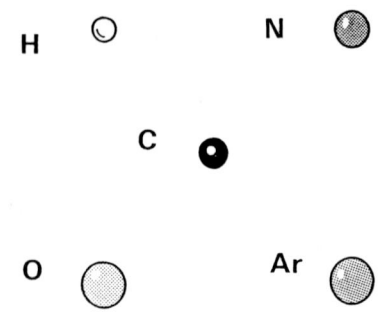

Chemical number 1 would be written as CO_2

Chemical number 7 would be written as N_2

  a How would each of chemicals 2 to 6 be written using chemical symbols?
  b Can you now give the *names* of each of the chemicals 1, 2, 3, 4, 5, 6 and 7?
  c For each of the chemicals you have just named, find out and write a little about its chemistry.

Chemical	Drawing	Is it an atom or a molecule?	Is it an element or a compound?
1			
2			
3			
4			
5			
6			
7			

© Borrows, Foster and Richardson 1991

Molecules in the air

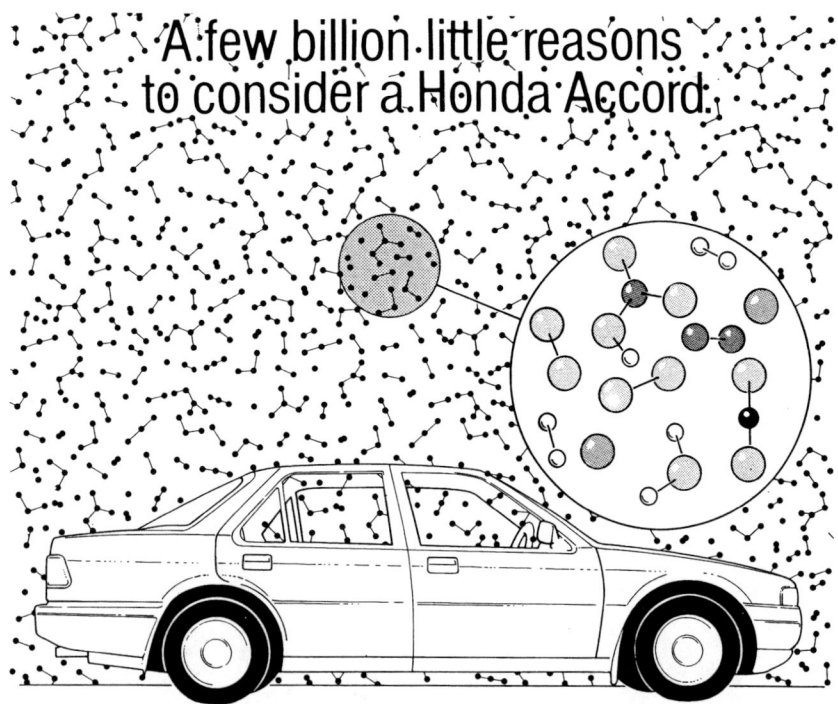

A few billion little reasons to consider a Honda Accord.

You don't drive a car in a vacuum. It, and you, are surrounded. By nitrogen, by oxygen, by argon, by rare compounds with strange names. In short, by that molecular soup we call air.

If that sounds like a statement of the obvious, then what follows is not. Air affects the performance of car and driver in a host of unexpected ways. Oxygen plays a vital role in the engine. Airborne corrosive agents like nitric acid can play havoc with your paintwork.

This is part of an advertisement for Honda cars. (The advertisement has been slightly modified, because the original was in colour). The advertiser is trying to show that air is a complicated mixture of elements and compounds, of atoms and molecules, which can affect cars in many ways.

An *element* cannot be split into anything simpler. It is made up of just one sort of atom,

For example or

Sometimes, these atoms may go around by themselves,

but more commonly they join together in pairs,

Two or more atoms joined together are called *molecules*. A *compound* is composed of two or more different sorts of atoms joined together to form molecules.

For example,  or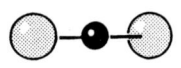

© Borrows, Foster and Richardson 1991

1 a The advertisement says we don't drive cars *in a vacuum*. What do we drive cars in?
   b Give *one* reason why cars would not work in a vacuum.

2 The advertisement mentions the *names* of four chemicals. One of these is nitric acid. Find the others, and then copy and complete this table:

Name of chemical	Is it an element or a compound?
Nitric acid	

3 a Explain why the advertisement talks about "A few <u>billion</u> <u>little</u> reasons". Be sure to comment on both of the underlined words.
   b In what way(s) is the drawing *not* a realistic representation of molecules in the air?

4 a You probably know the names of the main gases present in air. What are they? What percentage of each is there in normal air?
   b Air is one example of a mixture that occurs naturally. Give *two* more examples.

5 There are seven different chemicals (1, 2, ... 7) represented in the drawings in the advertisement. These are shown in the first two columns of the table below.
Copy the table carefully, and complete it.

6 It would be rather boring having to do these drawings all the time, so chemists often use a sort of shorthand. A chemical symbol consists of one or two letters. These are the symbols for the atoms shown in the advertisement:

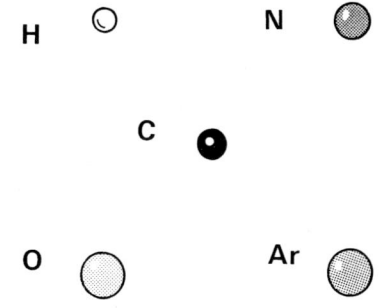

Chemical number 1 would be written as CO_2

Chemical number 7 would be written as N_2

   a How would each of chemicals 2 to 6 be written using chemical symbols?
   b Can you now give the *names* of each of the chemicals 1, 2, 3, 4, 5, 6 and 7?
   c For each of the chemicals you have just named, find out and write a little about its chemistry.

Chemical	Drawing	Is it an atom or a molecule?	Is it an element or a compound?
1			
2			
3			
4			
5			
6			
7			

© *Borrows, Foster and Richardson 1991*

INDEX

A
acceleration, 40
acid(s), 20, 31, 41
　rain, 25, 26
aerosol, 45
agar cultures, 56
aids, 54
air, 29
　conditioning, 56
　pollution, 24, 26
　pressure, 36
alcohol, 6
algae, 13
alkali(s), 20, 31
alpha
　radiation, 33
　rays, 34
alum, 15
ammonia, 31
anabolic steroids, 8
aperture, 49
argon, 19, 29
ASA number, 49
atom(s), 29, 33, 34

B
background radiation, 34
bacteria, 9, 58
　growth of, 10
balanced diet, 7
batteries, 41, 47
Ben Johnson, 40
beta
　radiation, 33
　rays, 34
biodegradable waste, 3
boiling point, 43

C
caffeine, 59
calcium carbonate, 25
camera, 49
cancer, 33
carbon, 24
　dioxide, 20, 24, 26, 45
　monoxide, 24, 26
catalyst, 26
cell, 41
Celsius, 43
CFCs, 5, 45
Chernobyl, 34
chlorine, 15, 16
chromosome, 11
coal, 24, 37, 38
compounds, 29
cook-chill food, 58
copper, 15

D
day and night, 53
degrees, 43
　Fahrenheit, 43
　of frost, 43
diet
　balanced, 7
　teeth and, 7
disasters, 36
DNA, 11
drugs, 8, 40
　social, 4, 6, 59

E
Earth, 52, 53
earthquake, 36
eclipse, 53
EEC beach standards, 48
electrons, 51
elements, 17, 29
electricity, 41, 44, 47
electromagnetic radiation, 42

electron, 51
electronic system, 48
endothermic, 47
energy, 39, 44, 47, 51, 52
　chain, 47
　kinetic,
　renewable source of, 39, 43, 44
evaporation, 43
exothermic, 47
extinction, 13
eye, 50

F
fast food, 14
fermentation, 6
film, 49
filtration, 20, 22
fizzy drinks, 22
flame test, 22
fluoride, 15
food, 47
　cook-chill, 58
　fast, 14
　poisoning, 9
force, 39
formulae, 30
fossil, 37
　fuels, 23, 24, 46
freezing
　point, 43
　temperatures, 43
fridge safety, 10
fuels, 23
　fossil, 23, 24, 46

G
gamma
　radiation, 33
　rays, 34
gases, 21, 30
gears, 39
Geiger counter, 34
genetics, 11
global warming, 45
greenhouse effect, 16, 45

H
haemophilia, 12
half-life, 35
heavy metals, 13
Hiroshima, 34
homosexual, 54
hormones, sex, 8
hydroelectric power, 44

I
igneous rock, 36, 37
incubation period, 56
indicator, 20, 31
infection, 54
infrared, 33
insulation, 45
isotope, 35

J
joules, 44
Jupiter, 52
Kaposi's sarcoma, 54
kilowatt, 44
kinetic energy, 39, 43

L
lead, 15
leaded petrol, 24
Legionnaires' disease, 56
lens, 49
levers, 39
light, 42, 48, 49
　-dependent resistor, 48
limestone, 37, 38

liquid, 21

M
metals, 17, 21, 27
metamorphic rock, 36, 37
methane, 45
microwave, 42, 58
Milky Way, 53
molecules, 29, 43
Moon, 36, 53
　phases of, 53

N
Neptune, 52
neutralisation, 20, 31
neutron, 34
nicotine, 4
nitrates, 13
nitrogen, 29
　oxides, 24, 26
non-biodegradable waste, 3
non-metals, 17
nuclear radiation, 33, 34
nucleus, 33, 34, 35

O
oil, 23, 24, 36
oxidation, 26
oxygen, 28, 29
ozone, 5, 45

P
parallel, 48
parasite, 3
Periodic Table, 17
petrol, 26
pH, 20
phases of the Moon, 53
phosphorus, 13
photosynthesis, 47
placenta, 4
planets, 52
plastic, 20, 27
pollution, 13, 16, 24, 26, 45
power, 44
proton, 34
puberty, 8

R
Radiation, 33, 34
　alpha, 33
　background, 34
　beta, 33
　electromagnetic, 42
　gamma, 33
　nuclear, 33, 34
　treatment, 33
　UV, 5
Radio, 42
Radioactive, 33, 34
　decay, 35
radioactivity, 34, 35
radioisotope, 33
rain forest, 14
rays
　alpha, 34
　beta, 34
　gamma, 34
raw materials, 23
reaction time, 40
recycling, 16, 45
reduction, 26
renewable source of energy, 44
reservoir, 15

retina, 51
rock
　igneous, 36, 37
　metamorphic, 36, 37
　sedimentary, 25, 36, 37
rust, 28
rusting, 27

S
salt, 28
satellite, 42
Saturn, 52
scientist, 51
sedimentary rock, 25, 36, 37
senses, 51
series, 48
sewage, 13
sex
　determination, 11
　hormones, 8
　-linked diseases, 12
shutter, 49
silica gel, 27
Sirius, 52
skin cancer, 5, 51
smoking, 4
social drugs, 4, 6, 59
soil, 20
solar system, 52
solid, 21
solute, 22
solution, 22
solvent, 22, 36
speed, 40
stationary orbit, 42
strata, 23, 37
street lamps, 48
stimulant, 59
sugar, 7
sulphur dioxide, 24, 26
Sun, 52, 53
　danger, 5
survey, 3, 10, 12, 16, 22, 28, 41, 48, 59

T
Teeth, 32
　decay, 7
　and diet, 7
toxicariasis, 3
turbine, 44

U
Uranus, 52
UV radiation, 5

V
variation, 12
virus, 51
volcanoes, 36, 37
voltage, 41
Voyager, 52

W
waste paper, 16
water, 15, 27
　pollution, 13
　to drink, 15
watt, 44
waves, 40
weather,
weight,
wind, 36
　chill factor, 43
wood pulp, 16
work, 39, 44

Social drugs – caffeine

A drug is any substance, which when taken, produces an effect on the mind or body.

Social drugs are legal drugs found in items such as tea, coffee, tobacco and alcohol. Social drugs, may harm the body if they are taken too frequently or in large quantities.

Caffeine is a social drug which is found in tea, coffee, cocoa and chocolate. It is often added to cola drinks and cold remedies.

Tea drinking began in the East and spread to the rest of the world. Some religious groups forbid the drinking of tea and coffee because they consider caffeine to be a dangerous drug. Caffeine is a stimulant which affects the central nervous system and brain. It increases alertness and the pulse rate. It causes extra water to be lost from the body due to increased urination.

Constant frequent drinking of tea and coffee can produce quite severe symptoms. Six cups of coffee or ten cups of tea drunk regularly every day may be a health risk. At this level caffeine may cause headaches, anxiety, diarrhoea and insomnia (unable to sleep).
Symptoms of caffeine withdrawal include nervousness, irritability and drowsiness. These may occur if people, who regularly drink tea or coffee, go without it for a day.

1 Caffeine is listed as an ingredient on the cola label but is not mentioned on the chocolate label. Suggest a reason for this.

2 Carry out a survey of the people in your home to find out:
  a How many caffeine-containing drinks are taken in one day
  Before you start you must design a survey sheet which might look something like this:)

Person	Number of cups/glasses per day		
	Tea	Coffee	Etc...
Mum	7	3	

b Why do the people in your family choose to drink these substances?

3 What does a drug like caffeine do when it acts as a *stimulant* on the body?

4 What could people drink instead of caffeine-containing products. Name as many drinks as you can.

5 Imagine you are a scientist employed by a coffee company to investigate the effect of caffeine on the body. You are provided with 100 people who are prepared to drink what you tell them.
Plan your experiment explaining what you would do and how you would record your results.

© Borrows, Foster and Richardson 1991

LISTERIOSIS

Listeria survives microwave tests

Fears about listeria have grown after reports that pregnant women who have eaten contaminated food have lost their babies because the bacteria can invade the womb. Infants and sick people are also vulnerable to the organism which thrives when shocked by extremes of temperature which have failed to kill it.

The researchers say that they injected two stuffed fresh chickens with listeria and cooked them for 38 minutes (10 per pound) in a domestic 650 watt microwave oven equipped with a turntable. Bacteria on the skin were destroyed but they survived in the stuffing where the temperature rose, in one case, to only 52°C.

Professor Richard Lacey, the Leeds University microbiologist, said yesterday that instructions for re-heating cook-chill foods are inadequate to protect consumers from infection.

Research he is due to publish in the Journal of Hospital Infection shows microwave cooking failed to kill listeria in four out of five cook-chill products tested.

"We injected 27 samples of foods with listeria and then followed the manufacturer's cooking instructions" he said. *"We found enough surviving listeria in 22 samples to cause disease. When we increased cooking times longer to kill the listeria the foods were dried out."*

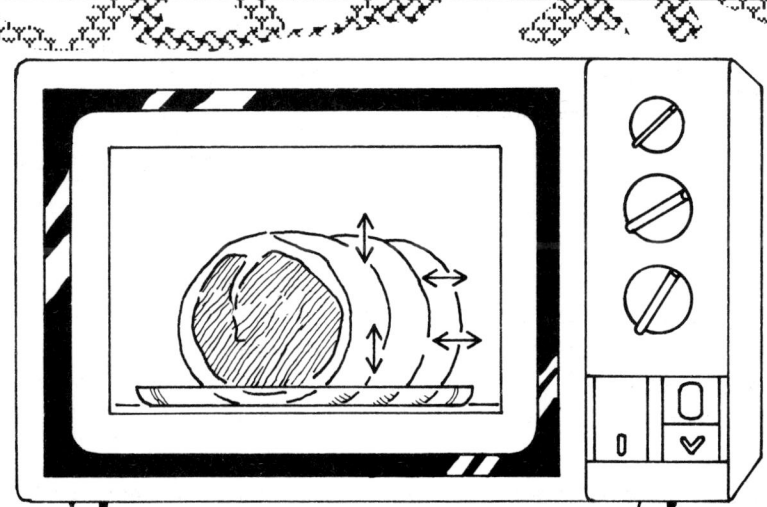

Food molecules vibrate, thus heating the food sample

1 For most people, Listeria bacteria cause flu-like symptoms which can be treated easily with antibiotics. However, some people are especially at risk. Name these people.

2 a The article goes on to quote the following observation on microwave cooking of chicken: *Bacteria on the skin were destroyed, but they survived in the stuffing, where the temperature rose, in one case, to only 52°C.*
What can you infer (guess why) from this observation.
b What experiment would you carry out to test one of your inferences?

3 In the instructions leaflet the manufacturer stresses *the need to leave food for the recommended standing time* after cooking in a microwave oven. Why is this important?

4 The article describes research which was due to be published in the *Journal of Hospital Infection*. Imagine you are the scientist who has done this work. Write a clear report of your work. Show the results in the form of a bar-chart.

5 Find out about other forms of food poisoning. Name the diseases that may occur and the foods which are often involved in spreading the disease.

6 A microwave is a type of short-wavelength radiation. It is produced by a magnetron which is housed inside the oven. Microwaves enter the food on all exposed surfaces. Metal surfaces reflect microwaves.
a What happens to molecules of food when microwaves enter the surface of food?
b Why should you *not* use tinfoil containers in a microwave oven?
c List some advantages of cooking with a microwave oven.

© Borrows, Foster and Richardson 1991

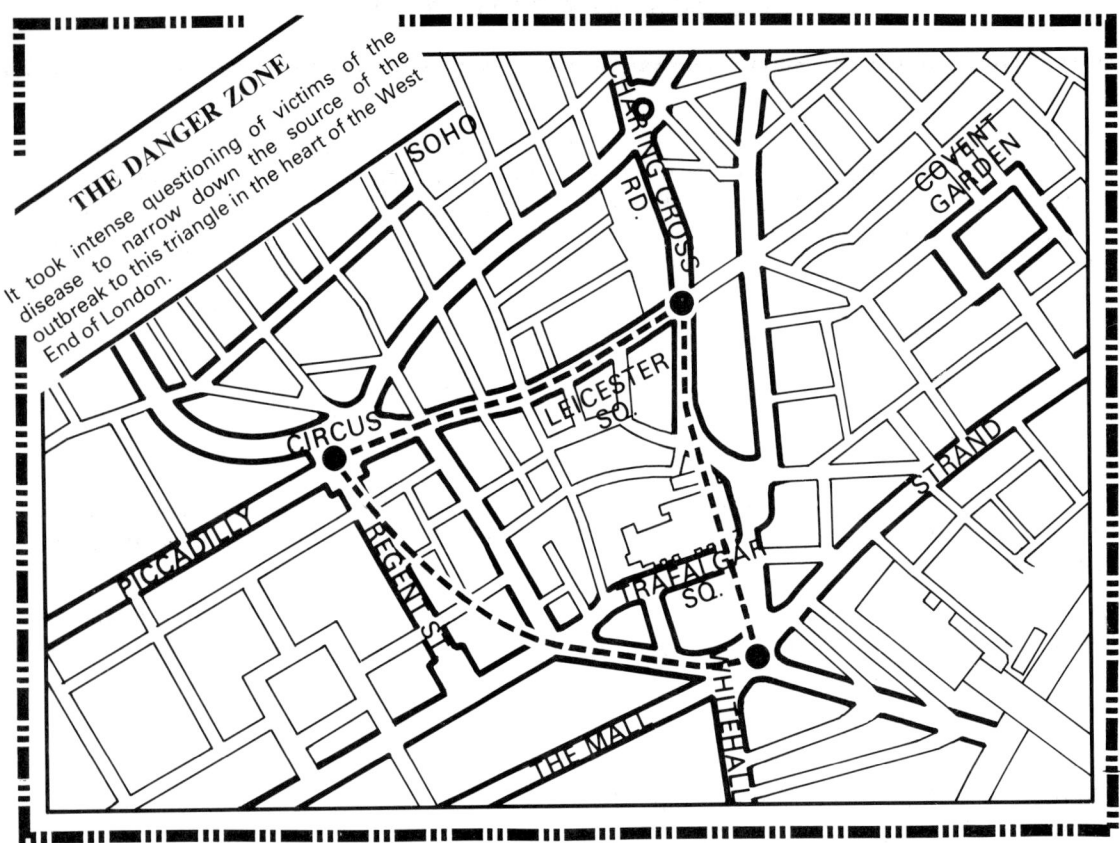

Figure 2

2 Imagine you are part of a team of Public Health inspectors trying to trace the source of an infection. You have been given the name of three patients who are suspected of suffering from Legionnaires' disease. The three people are in different hospitals, one in East London, one in West London and one in Kent.
   a Why would you question these people carefully and what would you want to find out?
   b Why would you study weather reports, describing temperature and wind direction, around the time of the outbreak?

3 The map shows the area under suspicion.
   a Name the boundaries of the area.
   b What investigations would scientists now carry out in this area?
   c Why would all doctors be warned to question any severely ill patients about their journeys during the previous ten days?
   d Find out what is meant by the term *incubation period*.

4 a Bacteria are a separate group of organisms from plants and animals. Suggest reasons why they are classified separately (Figure 1 on page 56 may provide some hints.)
   b Legionnella bacteria are *pathogenic* bacteria. Use a dictionary to find out what this means.
   c Find out how to carry out an experiment to investigate if a sample of water contains any bacteria.

5 Outbreaks of Legionnaires' disease in the United Kingdom are now becoming more common. As a result, MPs (Members of Parliament) discussed the issue on Tuesday 6 February 1989.
Imagine you are an MP for the area in which you live. Write down the things that you would want to discuss. Give reasons for discussing your items and outline your proposals for the future.
It may help you if you make your notes in the form of a table. Use the headings given below:

Parliamentary Meeting to discuss the outbreak of Legionnaires Disease. Agenda for meeting.

1 *Items for discussion*
2 *Reasons for discussing this item*
3 *Future proposals*

© *Borrows, Foster and Richardson 1991*

Killer in the city

Legionnaires' disease, a form of pneumonia, is caused by the bacterium *Legionella pneumophila*. This organism has been found to grow and multiply in water cooling tanks in air-conditioning systems. Legionella bacteria need special conditions to multiply – *first*, the presence of sludge, rust or algae on which the bacteria can feed and *second*, a water temperature of 20–45°C. These conditions can be prevented from occurring by cleaning and disinfecting water systems every spring and autumn, and by careful monitoring of water temperature.

The cooling tanks of most air-conditioning systems are usually situated on the roof of a building. Sprays of water, which are produced in the tank to cool the air, may be blown onto nearby streets below, during certain weather conditions.

The disease, which has an incubation period of 10 days, is difficult to diagnose because the symptoms are very similar to other forms of pneumonia. Failure to treat the disease quickly may lead to death.

Scientists are now able to grow (culture) the Legionella bacterium on agar. When the bacteria, which have been isolated from water systems, have grown, they can then be compared to the strain of bacteria isolated from infected patients. In this way, the source of an infection can be found.

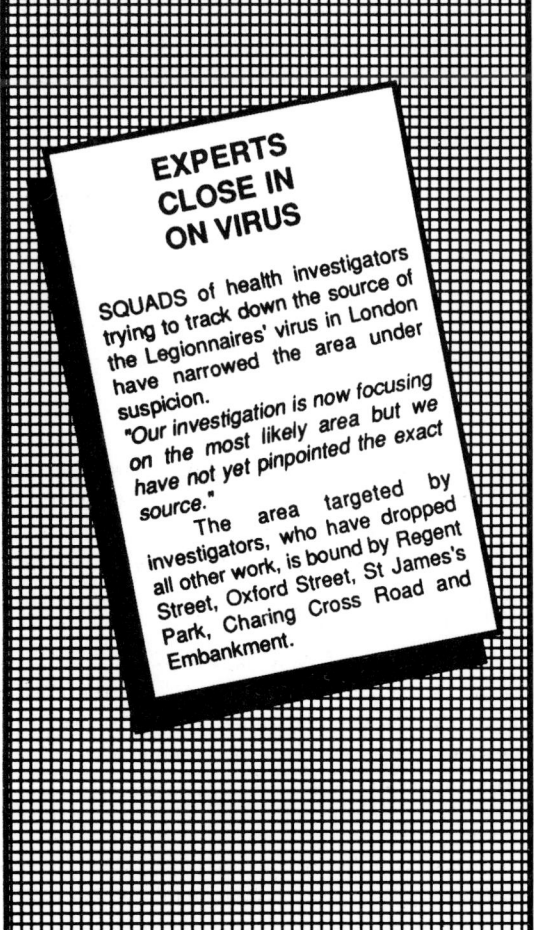

EXPERTS CLOSE IN ON VIRUS

SQUADS of health investigators trying to track down the source of the Legionnaires' virus in London have narrowed the area under suspicion.

"Our investigation is now focusing on the most likely area but we have not yet pinpointed the exact source."

The area targeted by investigators, who have dropped all other work, is bound by Regent Street, Oxford Street, St James's Park, Charing Cross Road and Embankment.

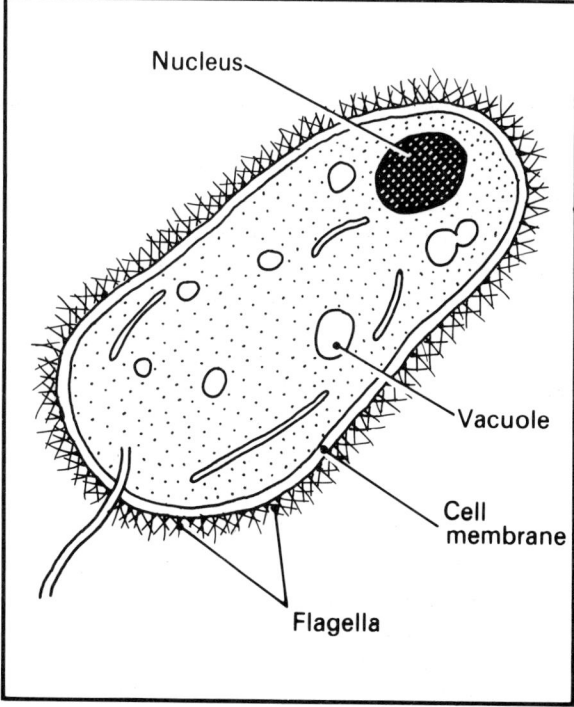

Figure 1

1 Read the main text again.
  a Name the type of organism that causes Legionnaires' disease.
  b Journalists do not always report science stories accurately. Can you spot the mistake in the first paragraph of the *Evening Standard* article.

© Borrows, Foster and Richardson 1991

TRACKING THE DISEASE

Health departments in the United States and the Public Health Laboratory Service (PHLS) in London began collecting evidence for the spread of Aids.

Year	Cases	Deaths
Pre 1981	76	63
1981	261	234
1982	999	853
1983	2764	2304
1984	5531	4251
1985	9475	5636
1986	9897	2960

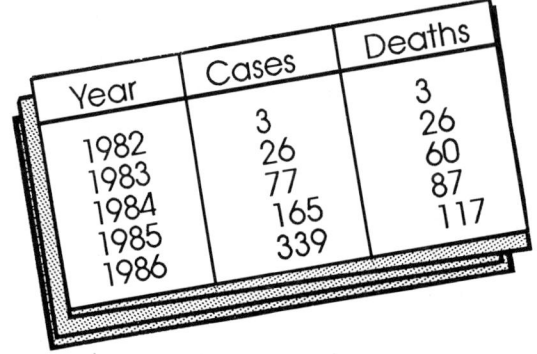

Year	Cases	Deaths
1982	3	3
1983	26	26
1984	77	60
1985	165	87
1986	339	117

1 Examine the *First* and *Second Reports* of the disease on page 54. What *two* pieces of evidence can be found in these reports to make scientists believe they were dealing with a *new* disease?

2 Draw a line graph to show the number of Aids cases in Britain between 1982 and 1986. Use this graph to estimate the number of cases in 1987.

3 Calculate the total number of Aids cases between 1981 and 1986, in the United States. Now calculate the number of deaths through Aids over the same period. What percentage of people died from the disease over this period?

4 The Starsky article on page 54 shows that Aids is not a disease that infects *only* homosexuals. How did the members of Paul Glaser's family contract Aids?

5 In an unpublished report by the Public Health Laboratory Service on March 31 1989 it was stated that 1624 drug abusers in Great Britain were suffering from Aids.
   a Why do you think that drug abusers run the risk of catching this disease?
   b Why do you think that 1624 may be a much lower figure than the actual number of drug abusers who carry the disease?

© *Borrows, Foster and Richardson 1991*

AIDS

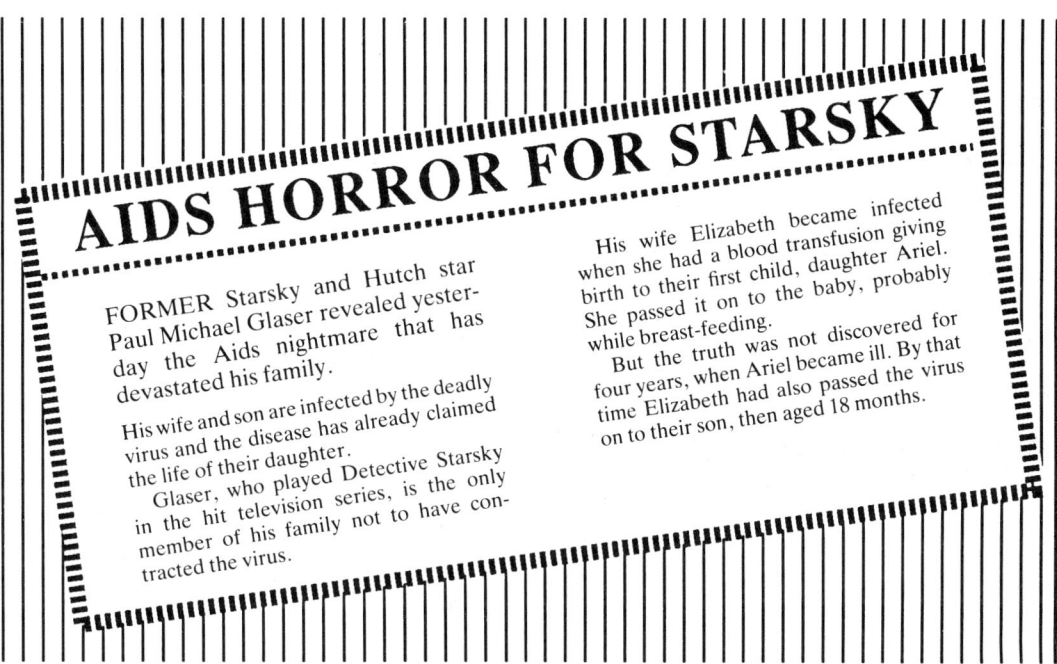

The acquired immune deficiency syndrome (AIDS) was first recognised in 1980.

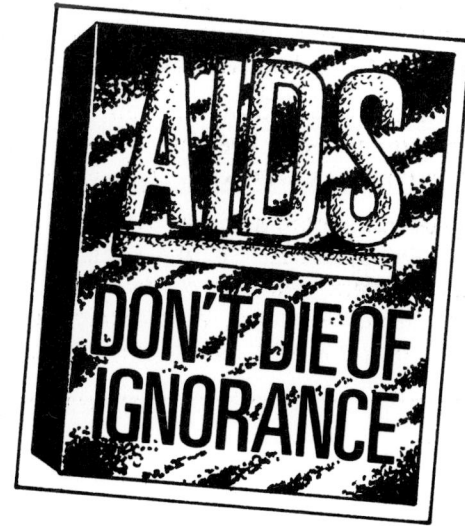

Acquired–caught not inherited

**Immune
Deficiency**–the body has little defence against infection

Syndrome–the group of illnesses that identify the disease.

The First Report of the Disease

The Centre for Disease Control (CDC) in Atlanta, Georgia reported five previously healthy homosexual men suffering from a rare form of pneumonia. Normally, this disease was seen only in people who were being treated with drugs which reduced their ability to fight off infections.

The Second Report

In 1981, 26 previously healthy young homosexuals in New York and California were reported to have developed a severe form of cancer called Kaposi's sarcoma. Usually this disease was seen only in elderly patients.

turn

© *Borrows, Foster and Richardson 1991*

Moon and Earth

1 List in order, with the largest first and the smallest last: Earth, Milky Way, Moon, Sun.

2 Figure 1 shows the Earth spinning on its axis and rays of light coming from the Sun. The axis of the Earth is tilted.
  a Copy Figure 1 and on it, shade a region of the Earth which is in sunlight all day long.
  b Which season is it, in the Northern hemisphere, in Figure 1?
  c The place marked X is Dakar in Senegal in West Africa. Can you find it in an atlas or on a globe? Explain how day and night occurs in Dakar and estimate the number of hours you would expect each to be.

3 When we see the moon and planets shining at night it is because they are reflecting light from the Sun. Figure 2 shows the orbit of the Moon in relation to the Earth and the Sun.

  a Assuming that the Earth does not block rays of sunlight from reaching the Moon, the Moon will look (from the Earth) like the shapes in Figure 3, at various times during a month. Copy Figure 3 and label each picture P, Q, R, S according to where you think the Moon will be at each stage.

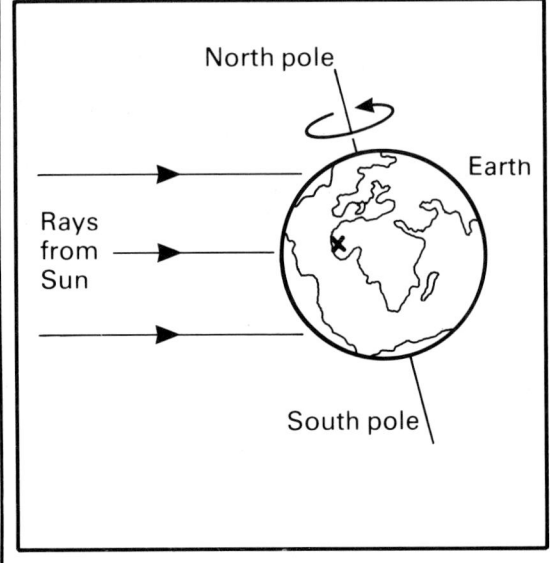

Figure 1

  b At what point (P, Q, R or S) is it possible that the Moon casts a shadow on the Earth (an *eclipse* of the Sun)?
  c At what point (P, Q, R or S) is it possible that the Earth casts a shadow on the Moon (an *eclipse* of the moon)?

Figure 2

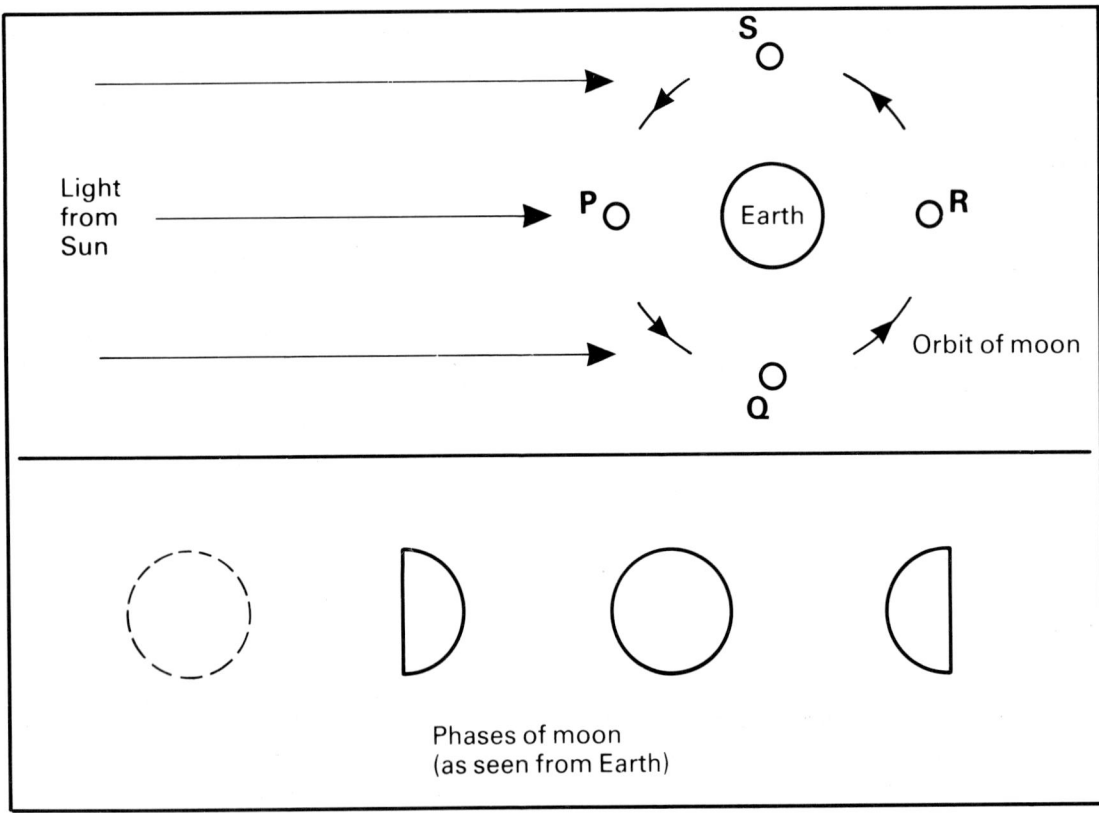

Phases of moon
(as seen from Earth)

© Borrows, Foster and Richardson 1991

Figure 3

VOYAGER 2

VOYAGER'S AMAZING JOURNEY INTO SPACE

SPACESHIP Voyager 2 was just one second late yesterday after travelling 4.5 billion miles to reach the edge of our solar system. It has hurtled through space for 12 years at the rate of one million miles a day. But it was in position to send back historic pictures of Neptune and re-write the science textbooks.

"We are exploring new worlds here," declared an astronomer as the icy planet and its previously uncharted moons were revealed.

Since its launch on September 20, 1977, the fragile craft has swept in a huge "slingshot effect" arc to explore the planets Jupiter, Saturn and Uranus. Rather than blasting the spaceship on its journey with rocket motors, scientists were able to take advantage of a line up of planets that happens just once every 176 years to help catapult the craft through space. As it soared past each planet it "stole" energy from their gravitational fields.

Voyager's journey of exploration is a once in a lifetime experience. It will be more than 170 years before a similar alignment of planets will occur again. In the early hours of yesterday morning the ship neared Neptune. Scientists have succeeded in coaxing the primitive electronics on board to send back pictures of breathtaking detail. Its faint radio signals are beamed to earth from a 12 foot dish using a radio transmitter that is no more powerful than the light bulb in a fridge.

Thanks to Voyager 2, a snip at £400 million for the mission, we now know a great deal more about Neptune. The planet, which is 56 times bigger than Earth, is so far from the Sun that it gets only 1,000th of the light that the Earth does. It is blasted by 400 mph winds in its atmosphere of methane, the familiar natural gas piped to homes throughout the country.

This intensely cold planet is a soft blue colour that gives it a calm appearance that conceals the truth of huge, violent hurricane-like storms. One single dark-spot storm pictured by Voyager 2 was itself large enough to swallow up the Earth.

On its journey the ship has travelled a curving path calling at Jupiter in 1979, Saturn in 1981 and Uranus in 1986. When it leaves Triton, Voyager will plunge into the depths of space, next stop the star Sirius, nearly 300,000 years away.

---

1 a List all the planets of the solar system from the Sun outwards. Place a tick against those which Voyager 2 has visited (you may include the Earth).

   b Copy the following table and use the press cutting above to complete it:

The journey of Voyager 2

Date	Planet	My age at that time

2 a Why was September 1977 chosen as the launch date for the Voyager 2 mission?

   b The space-craft did not use rocket engines to get from planet to planet. What force did it latch on to?

   c On leaving the solar system, Voyager 2 will be heading for the star Sirius. Use a reference book to find out another name for this star and say why it is so called.

3 What were the main discoveries made by Voyager 2 about the planet Neptune?

4 Since 1977 when Voyager 2 took off, there have been many advances in technology. For example, the compact disc player did not come into common use until 1983.

By discussion with parents or other adults, make out a list of everyday things in the home or elsewhere that have only come into common use since 1977. For each item listed, say why you think it was not available fifty years earlier. For example, you might say because of modern electronics or new materials.

5 a According to the press cutting, what was the cost of the Voyager 2 mission?

   b If you estimate that a new comprehensive school costs £10 million and a new hospital costs £100 million, do you think that the Voyager 2 mission was good value for money? Give arguments for and against spending money on space research.

© Borrows, Foster and Richardson 1991

The eye and laser surgery

Atoms are made up of a nucleus surrounded by electrons moving around it. Sometimes an electron can move further away from the nucleus. This increases the energy in the atom and it is called an *excited* atom. When the electron moves back to its original level, energy is released in the form of light.

In a laser this light energy moves along a ruby rod. If this hits another excited atom, even more light is released. The light bounces off mirrors at each end of the rod, gaining more and more energy. Eventually, the intense light shoots out of the semi-transparent mirror. This is called a laser beam.

Lasers are used to weld torn retinas in the eye. They are also used to destroy cancer cells.

Figure 1

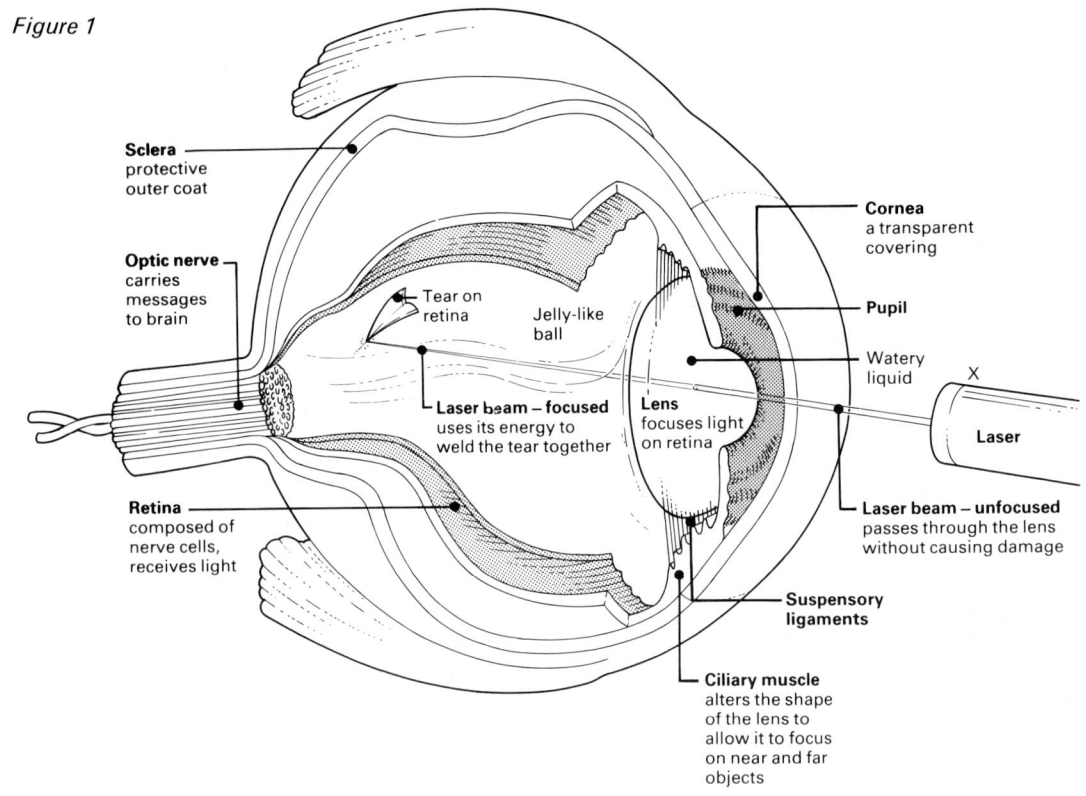

1 a Describe how it is possible for the laser to weld the retina without damaging the lens.
  b Removal of cancer cells using a laser beam allows the patient to recover faster than if the cells had been cut out using a scalpel. Explain the reason for this.

2 a When light passes into the eye it travels through several structures before hitting the retina. Describe the route taken by light travelling to the retina starting from point X as shown in Figure 1. (Remember that light travels in straight lines.)
  b Why does damage to the retina cause blindness?
  c Some people are born blind. The retina of the eye, however, may be undamaged. What other parts of the eye could cause blindness if they are not working properly?

3 The eye is important to a scientist because many observations are made using sight.
  a What other senses can the scientist use to make observations?
  b Why is it so important for a scientist to make careful observations?
  c What does a scientist normally do with the observations she/he has made.
  d Imagine that you are a scientist who has observed that when light hits a shiny surface, it bounces off, but if it enters a transparent material, such as glass, it passes through and bends as it passes.

  Plan some simple experiments you could do in the laboratory to investigate this. Write down all the apparatus you would use.

© Borrows, Foster and Richardson 1991

The Snappit camera has a fixed lens, a fixed aperture and a single shutter speed. In better quality cameras, the lens will move outwards to focus on near objects and inwards to focus on distant objects; the aperture will be of variable size, to let in more or less light, and there will be a choice of shutter speeds.

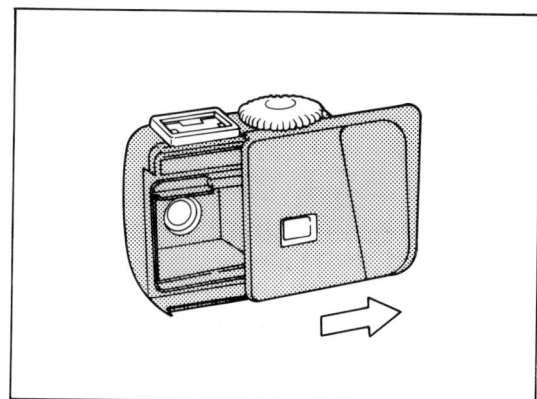

1 Slide off the back of your camera in the direction shown

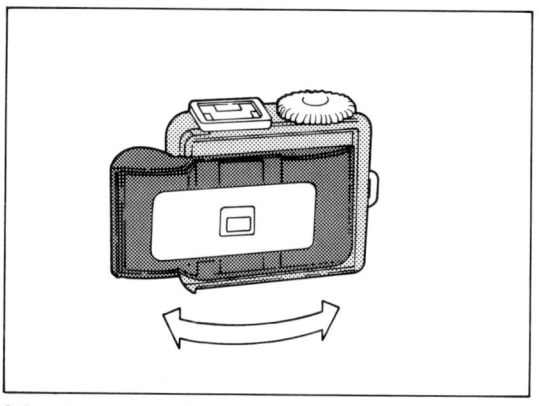

2 Snap in your snappit film and replace the back of your camera

3 Rotate the film wind on knob anticlockwise until the exposure reader shows 1. Flip up the viewfinder before taking any photos.

3 a Do you need a wide or a narrow aperture if the lighting conditions are poor?

b Do you need a fast or a slow shutter speed to *freeze* a picture of a moving racing car.

4 The human eye is like a camera in some ways. Both have a lens, for example.

a In the eye, what is like the aperture in a camera?

b In the eye, what is like the film in a camera?

5 Describe how you could carry out an experiment to measure the shutter speed of a Snappit camera. One approach might involve an electronic sensor, such as you might have used with a computer or microelectronics kit. Another approach might involve photographing a moving object. Or you might be able to think of something better.

Include a diagram of what you would do. Describe what measurements you would make and say how you would work out the result.

© *Borrows, Foster and Richardson 1991*

SNAPPIT

The earliest cameras, made in the 1850s, were large, cumbersome affairs. Photographic *plates* had to be prepared with wet chemicals whenever a picture was to be taken. Only still objects could be photographed because the plates needed long exposure times.

Nowadays, cameras are small and cheap. The illustration shows a *Snappit* camera which is given away free when you get films developed. Like most modern cameras, it uses prepared film in a cassette in place of the wet plates of old. But the principle of the camera remains the same. A lens focuses light from the subject onto the light sensitive film. This happens when the *shutter* opens for a short time.

Figure 1 shows how a camera focuses light from a distant object onto the film.

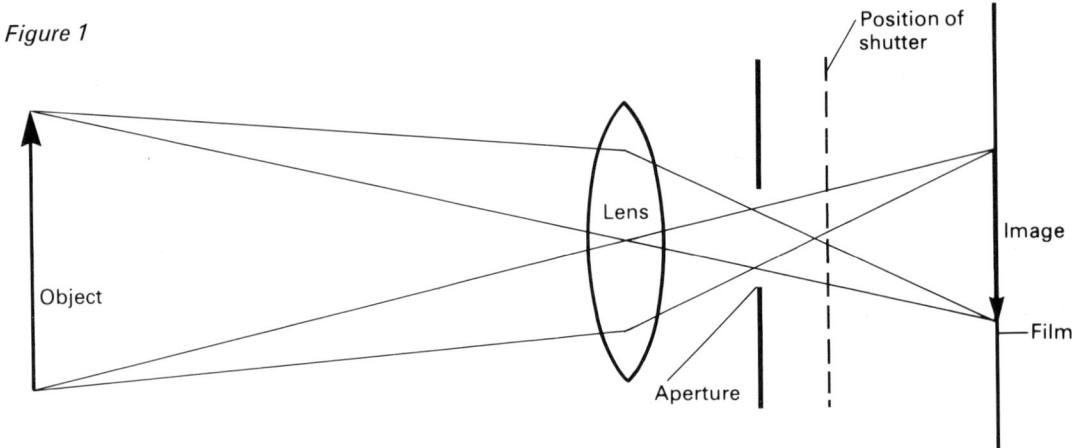

Figure 1

1 a Which part of the camera focuses the light?
 b Which part of the camera allows light in for a brief time?
 c What do we call the hole through which the light enters the camera?

2 Early Victorian cameras did not have a shutter. To take a photo, the photographer would simply remove the lens cover for so many seconds and then replace it.

 a Why were fast shutters not required in early cameras?

Modern cameras use film whose *speed* is rated by what is called an *ASA* number. For example, normal film is rated at 100 ASA but a higher speed film is rated at 400 ASA.

 b Which film would be best for taking indoor photos, without using a flash, 100 ASA or 400 ASA?

turn

© *Borrows, Foster and Richardson 1991*

LAMP-POSTS

1 Some street lamps give an orange coloured light, others a purple colour and others an almost white colour.

   a Carry out a survey of street lights near your home. Record what colour light they give and which type of lamp-post they are.

   b Do you notice any pattern in the type of lamp-post and the colour of the light it gives?

2 Show, with a sketch, how a street lamp uses a reflector to direct the light downwards.

3 Lamps may be joined in a circuit in two ways:

- in series:

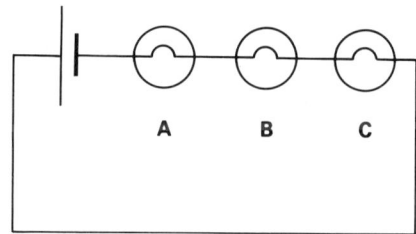

- in parallel:

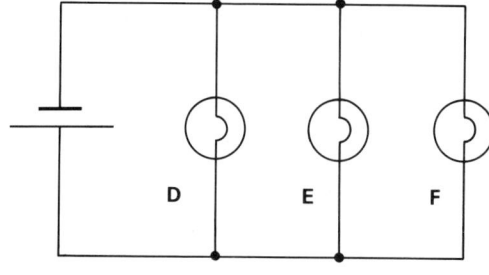

   a What would happen to lamps B & C if lamp A were to blow?

   b What would happen to lamps E & F if lamp D were to blow?

   c Do you think that street lights are joined *in series* or *in parallel*? Explain.

4 Shown below is a simple electronic system for controlling a street light. The lamp is switched *on* when no light falls on the sensor and is switched *off* when light does fall on it. The sensor is a light dependent resistor. It is normally situated in the little dome seen on top of the street lamp.

Explain how this system switches the lamp on at night and off in the day time.

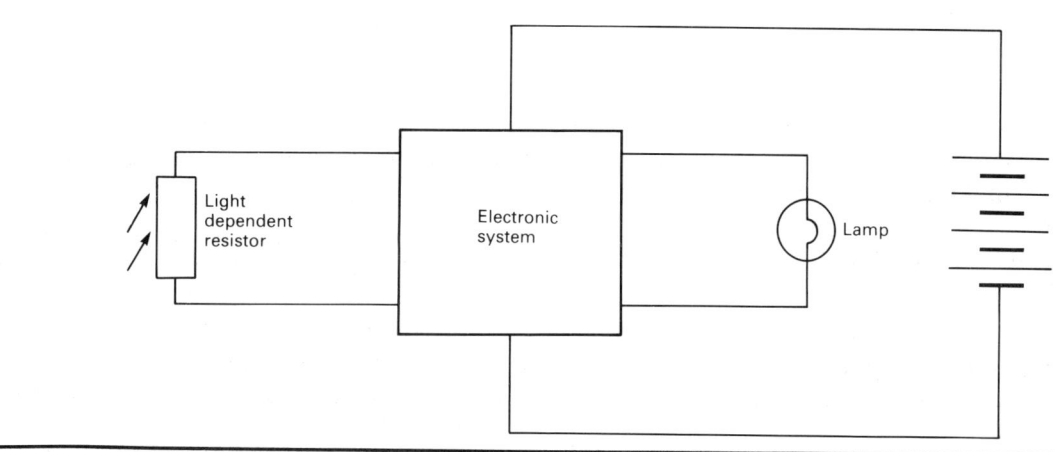

© Borrows, Foster and Richardson 1991

BIRD SCARER

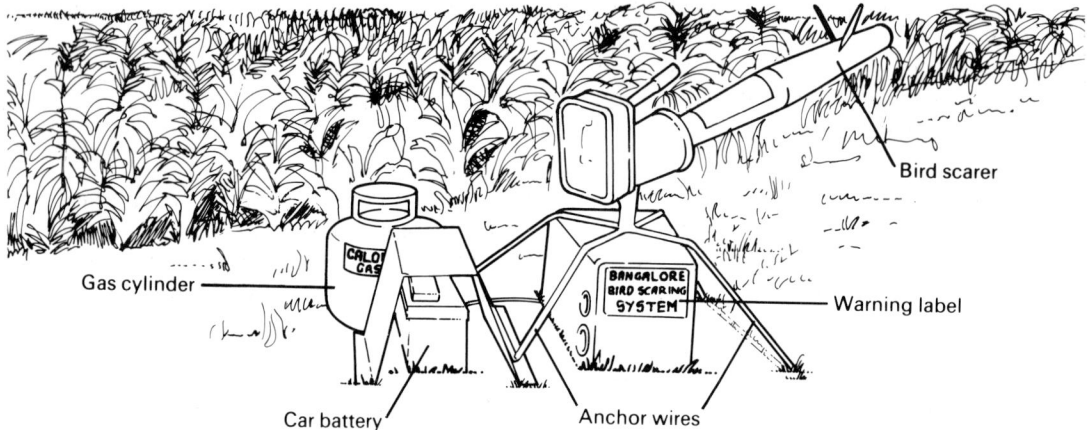

Look at this picture of a bird scarer on the edge of a field of corn. Farmers often use such devices in an attempt to prevent birds eating too much of their crops. Every few minutes it gives a very loud bang, scaring away any birds that have started to eat the seeds.

Much of this assignment is about energy. Remember, energy cannot be created or destroyed, only changed from one form to another. Here, to remind you, is a list of some forms of energy.

Sound,   Chemical,

Electrical,   Kinetic (movement),

Nuclear,   Potential (up hill)

Heat,

1 a The birds eat the corn as food. The corn contains stored energy. In what form is the energy stored?
b The birds will turn the stored energy of the corn into what form(s) of energy when they eat it?
c Where did the energy that is stored in the corn actually come from?
d What name is given to the process in which energy is stored up in corn and other plants?

2 a Look at the picture of the bird scarer itself. You should be able to see (at least) *two* sources of stored chemical energy. What are they?
b The Calor gas is burnt, forming carbon dioxide and water. Is this reaction endothermic or exothermic?
c The burning gas heats up the surrounding air rapidly, which in turn causes a loud noise. Copy this energy chain and complete it.

...energy → ...energy → ...energy
(calor gas)

d Energy can be neither created nor destroyed, so what happens to the energy at the end of this chain? Where does it go to?

e The car battery supplies electricity, which in turn gives a spark which ignites the Calor gas. Write an energy chain for this process.

3 a Plan an investigation to see whether the sort of bird-scarer shown above really works. Does it really stop the crops being eaten? Say exactly what you would do in your investigation, and be particularly careful to make sure it is a fair test.
b Even if the bird-scarer *does* actually drive away the birds, it may not be financially worthwhile. The value of the crops saved from the birds might not balance the cost of buying the bird-scarer, and the running costs of the Calor gas and the battery.
How would you try to investigate this?

4 a What other ways have been used to scare away birds, in this country or elsewhere, now or in the past?
b Can you invent a bird scarer, suitable for a gardener who wants to keep the birds away from a small garden? Use only things that are readily available to you.
Draw a diagram of your bird-scarer, and write a few sentences explaining how it works.

© Borrows, Foster and Richardson 1991

On the 26th April 1989 a meeting was held at 10 Downing Street to discuss the risks of climatic change and global warming. In the past 80 years the average temperature has increased by half a degree Celsius.

Burning fossil fuel (coal, gas, oil and wood) uses oxygen and produces carbon dioxide. However, trees use carbon dioxide and release oxygen. So, there should be a healthy balance. But, over the last 150 years more fossil fuel has been burnt and more forests have been cut down and burnt. Both processes release carbon dioxide which has increased in the atmosphere by 24% over the past 150 years.

When shortwave radiation from the sun reaches the earth it is absorbed but some of it is lost back into space as longwave *heat* radiation. This is trapped by the carbon dioxide, which then makes the climate warmer. A greenhouse works in the same way, with the longwave radiation being trapped by the glass. Other greenhouse gases include CFCs and methane.

Name of gas	Products which release this gas	Methods used by Grant family to cut down release of gas

1 a Name the *three* greenhouse gases mentioned in the article and write them in the above table.

For each gas, write down how Man's actions have increased the amount of gas in the environment. List the ways in which the Grant family have tried to minimize the release of these gases.

2 a What percentage of the 47 tonnes of pollution do the Grant family produce *directly*?
  b The article suggests that the Grant family could cut down the 5.5 tonnes of carbon dioxide produced through their central heating by 15%. How much carbon dioxide would they then produce?
  c How could the family make the 15% saving described in **b**?

3 a Why do plants need carbon dioxide?
  b How is the carbon that is stored in the plant, returned to the air?
  c Plants release oxygen to the atmosphere. Why is this gas important for animals?

4 The greenhouse effect has caused the average temperatures to increase. What worrying effects is this having on the environment?

5 Conduct a survey in your own home.
  a List all the products that have been bought for the home. (Look carefully at the labels on products.)
  b List all the activities, carried out by family members, that release greenhouse gases.
  c Write down the ways in which you could cut down the amounts of greenhouse gases released in your home.

© *Borrows, Foster and Richardson 1991*

The greenhouse effect

- **The Grant family believe they are environmentally conscious but, like all of us, they would have to do a great deal more before having any real impact in the fight against pollution.**

The fact that they have children has made them think even harder about what sort of world they will leave for the next generation, and they are worried particularly about the hole in the ozone layer and the effects of global warming.

They have stopped using aerosols because of the damage to the ozone layer caused by chlorofluorocarbons (CFCs) and because there are other environmental problems caused by CFC substitutes.

Instead, they use roll-on deodorants, but they are still probably pumping about half a tonne a year of CFCs into the atmosphere, because of other goods and services they use, such as insulation material, foam-sprayed packaging and dry-cleaning.

The Grants have a modern well-insulated house, with double glazing and draught-proofing, which makes their heating more efficient.

Although their gas central heating is more efficient than average, they have no cavity wall insulation and are still probably losing at least 20% of the heat. With that and other minor improvements, they could reduce the 5.5 tonnes of carbon dioxide produced from heating by 10–15% at an extra cost of perhaps £400, which would be recovered within three years. Their four tonnes of carbon dioxide from electricity use could be significantly reduced by energy-efficient bulbs, which are more expensive to buy but cheaper in the long term.

When they buy food and other goods, the Grants try to avoid taking home unnecessary packaging and try to use plastic bags from supermarkets more than once. But they are still probably contributing about 2.5 tonnes of methane, another greenhouse gas, to atmospheric pollution because of the waste they produce, which is tipped in landfill sites and then leaks back into the environment. That could probably be reduced by a third if they cut out even more unnecessary packaging, recycled some of their rubbish and did not allow food to go to waste.

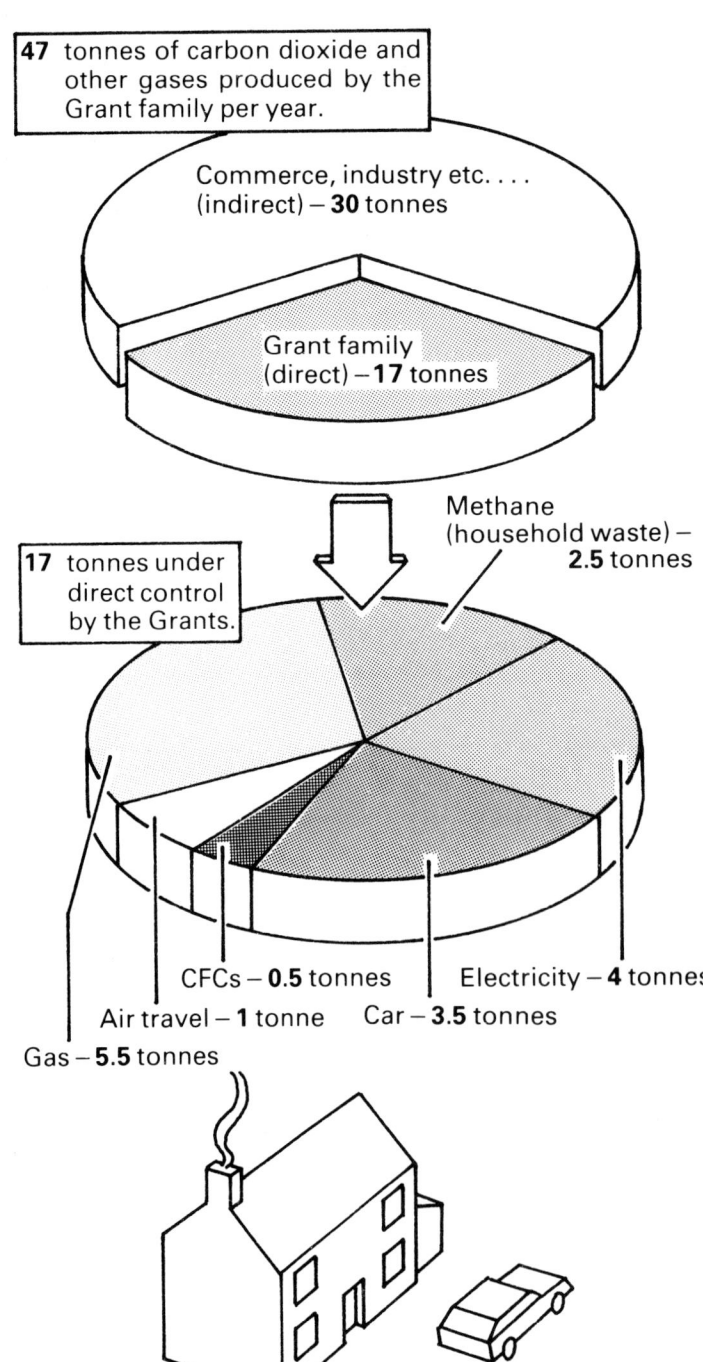

© Richard Palmer. The Sunday Times 24th September 1989

© Borrows, Foster and Richardson 1991

Electricity for free?

TECHNOLOGY, designed to impress a Russian Czar 150 years ago, is being used by the Duke of Devonshire to cut his annual electricity bill by £40,000. In 1844 the then Duke was anxious to impress Czar Nicholas on a State visit to Britain. Inspired by his gardener, Joseph Paxton, who later built the Crystal Palace in London, the Duke had an artificial lake dug in the hills above Chatsworth House in Derbyshire. A 15-inch bore pipe was then laid ten feet underground from the lake to his garden half a mile away. Water rushing down the pipe powered a 90 m high fountain, easily the highest in the world. In 1893 the system was extended to supply the house with electricity but this fell into disuse in the 1930s. The present Duke has now installed a new turbine which is run by the 5000 litres of water that thunder every minute down the refurbished pipes from three lakes in the hills. The scheme should pay for itself in three years. Visitors to Chatsworth, one of Britain's finest stately homes, won't be aware of the changes but the original fountain is still there for all to see.

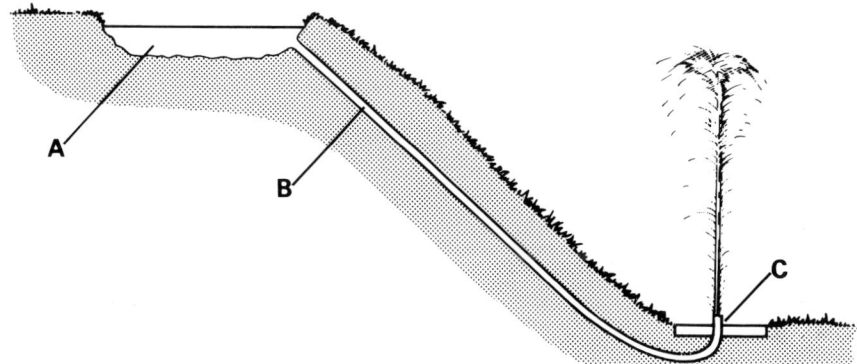

1 The diagram shows how the Chatsworth fountain obtained water from the lake. Name the parts labelled A, B & C.

2 What kind of energy is represented by
   a the water stored in the lake?
   b the water rushing out of the mouth of the fountain?
   c the water at the top of the fountain?

3 Was the lake more than or less than 90 metres above the garden? Explain your answer.

4 a What additional equipment was needed to generate electricity from the water flow?
   b Where was this equipment installed?

5 Give: **a** some advantages and **b** some disadvantages of generating electricity this way as opposed to a coal fired power station.

6 We can calculate work done (in joules) using the equation
work done (J) = weight (N) × height (m)
   a If 1 litre of water weighs 10 N, what is the weight of the 5000 litres which the bore pipe delivers in a minute?
   b How much work would be done if this weight of water is raised 90 metres (the height of the possible fountain)?
   c If this work is done every *minute*, how much work is done per *second*?

The answer to **c** is the power supplied by the falling water. Another word for joules per second (J/s) is watts (W). To change your answer into kilowatts (kW), divide your last answer by 1000. This gives how many kW? This is the power supplied to the Chatsworth turbine, which turns a dynamo (generator) to generate electricity.

   d Not all the power supplied by the water is converted to electrical power. Explain where the power is "wasted".

7 The Chatsworth project is a small scale *hydro-electric* power station. Like wave power and wind power, such a source is called a *renewable* source of energy. All renewable energy sources receive their energy from the sun.
   a Why do we refer to the Chatsworth hydro-electric scheme as a renewable source of energy?
   b Explain how the electrical energy at Chatsworth ultimately comes from the sun.

© Borrows, Foster and Richardson 1991

FREEZING TEMPERATURES

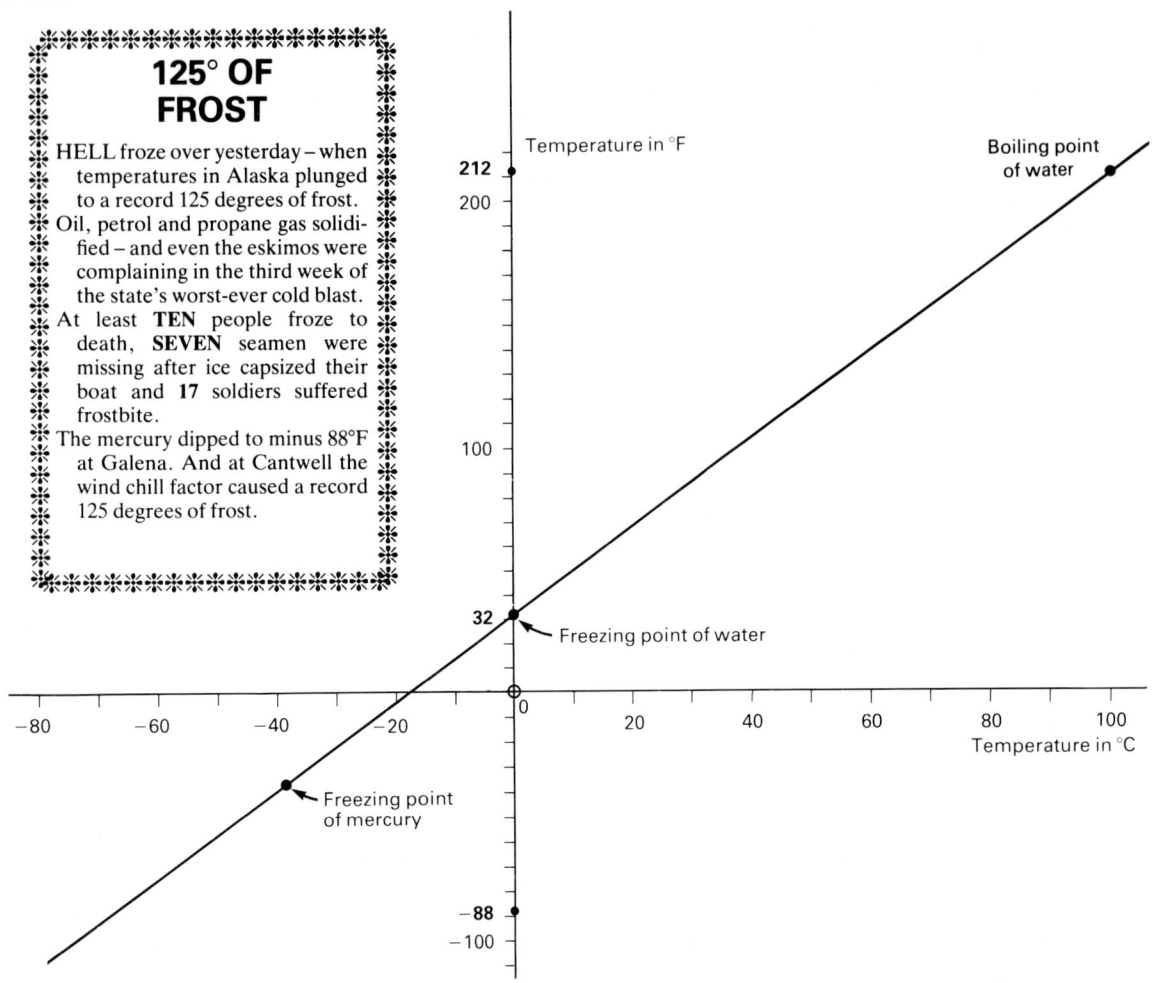

125° OF FROST

HELL froze over yesterday – when temperatures in Alaska plunged to a record 125 degrees of frost. Oil, petrol and propane gas solidified – and even the eskimos were complaining in the third week of the state's worst-ever cold blast.

At least **TEN** people froze to death, **SEVEN** seamen were missing after ice capsized their boat and **17** soldiers suffered frostbite.

The mercury dipped to minus 88°F at Galena. And at Cantwell the wind chill factor caused a record 125 degrees of frost.

The graph may be used to convert temperatures in degrees Fahrenheit (°F) to degrees of Celsius (°C).

When a liquid evaporates it cools down because the fast-moving molecules, which escape from the surface of the liquid, take with them kinetic energy. The molecules left in the liquid have less energy and the liquid is therefore cooler. Blowing air over the surface of the liquid makes it evaporate quicker. More fast-moving molecules are helped to escape, so the liquid cools even more.

---

1 a The freezing point of water is 0°C. What is this in °F?
  b What is −88°F in °C?

2 The number of "degrees of frost" is the number of degrees below the freezing point of water on the Fahrenheit scale.
  a What was the temperature in Cantwell in °F? (Last sentence of newspaper cutting).
  b On a day in London when the temperature was −5°C, how many degrees of frost was this?

3 a What is meant by the expression "the mercury dipped to −88°F"?
  b Does the expression make sense? Give a reason for your answer.

c From the press cutting above, what can you say about the freezing point of propane?

4 a Design an experiment to test the hypothesis that when air is blown across a damp surface the temperature of the surface drops. Include a labelled diagram of your experiment, say what you would do and say how you would obtain the result.
  b Explain what you think is meant by *wind chill factor*.

5 In view of the risk of the wind chill factor, what advice would you give to people walking in the hills when the weather is uncertain?

© Borrows, Foster and Richardson 1991

SATELLITE T.V.

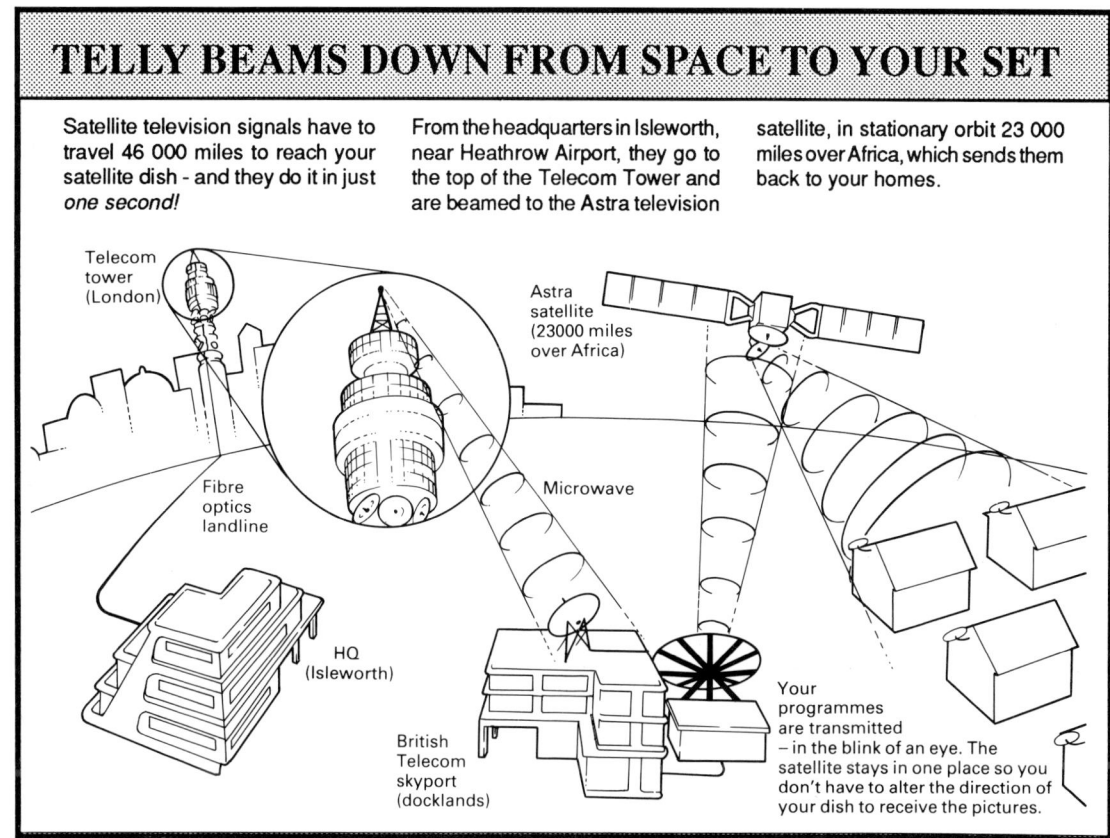

TELLY BEAMS DOWN FROM SPACE TO YOUR SET

Satellite television signals have to travel 46 000 miles to reach your satellite dish - and they do it in just *one second*!

From the headquarters in Isleworth, near Heathrow Airport, they go to the top of the Telecom Tower and are beamed to the Astra television satellite, in stationary orbit 23 000 miles over Africa, which sends them back to your homes.

Your programmes are transmitted — in the blink of an eye. The satellite stays in one place so you don't have to alter the direction of your dish to receive the pictures.

Light, microwaves, radio and TV waves are all types of electromagnetic radiation. They consist of vibrations which travel through space at 300 million metres per second (186 000 miles per second).

1 a In what form of electromagnetic radiation does the TV signal travel from Isleworth to the Telecom tower?
  b In what form of electromagnetic radiation does the signal travel from the Telecom tower to the docklands skyport?

2 Radiation travels through space from earth to the satellite and back.
  a How many miles does electromagnetic radiation travel through space in 1 second?
  b Why is the newspaper wrong in the above article?

3 a What is meant by a satellite being in *stationary orbit*?
  b To receive satellite TV you need a *dish* aerial which points at the satellite. What would the dish have to do if the satellite were not in stationary orbit?
  c Is the moon in stationary orbit?

4 The radius of the Earth is about 4000 miles.
  a How far above the surface of the Earth is the Astra satellite?
  b What, therefore, is the radius of the satellite's orbit?
  c Assume that the satellite is directly over the equator and over the same line of longitude as London (ie 0 degrees).
  On a sheet of A4 paper turned "sideways", and using a scale of 1 cm = 1000 miles, draw a circle at the far left hand side of the paper to represent the Earth. Imagine this to be a vertical section through London (0° longitude). Label the North Pole, the South Pole, the Equator and London (51.5° north of the Equator). Now put on the position of the satellite.
  Draw in a line with arrows on it showing the TV signal travels from London to the satellite and back to a house in London.

5 Imagine that you wish to send a message (a birthday greeting, say) to a friend who lives across the road from where you live. List 10 ways in which you could send this message. For each way, say whether the message is sent by means of an object or by means of a vibration.

© Borrows, Foster and Richardson 1991

BATTERIES

Most homes have lots of battery powered devices...

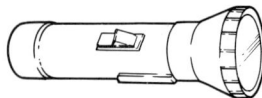  

and there are many different types of "batteries"...

Strictly speaking, in most cases we shouldn't be talking about batteries at all. We should call them *cells*. A cell is the thing that actually makes the electricity, by means of a chemical reaction. The *voltage* that you get from a cell depends upon which chemical reaction takes place.

A battery case has to be quite tough to prevent the chemicals from leaking out. Some batteries contain acids, and others contain very poisonous chemicals. A commonly used chemical reaction gives about 1.5 volts.

Cells may be joined together to form a "battery of cells", or battery for short. A 4.5 volt battery will actually have three 1.5 volt cells joined together, and wrapped up so that it looks like one single cell. You could use three separate 1.5 volt cells but they might not fit so easily into place. It might be difficult also to connect them together in the right way. We need batteries with different voltages because different devices need different voltages to operate them.

At one time, nearly all cells were of the zinc/carbon type. But now you also may get alkaline/manganese cells. These tend to last longer. Where a small size is important, for example in hearing aids, there may be a mercury cell.

Increasingly, people are using re-chargeable cells. These contain special chemicals. If you connect them up to a re-charger, the original chemical reaction is reversed, and the "flat" battery gets its power back. Never attempt to re-charge ordinary batteries. It could be very dangerous. Car batteries (lead/acid accumulators) are a special type of re-chargeable battery.

1 Carry out a survey of battery powered devices in your home. Draw up a table to record your findings, making clear how many batteries are in each device, their total voltage, and the type of batteries used.

2 Alex bought a battery for his radio, but when he got it home, it seemed to be wet around the end. He took it back to the shop because he thought that acid might be leaking out. The shop keeper said it was only the glue.
   a How would you test the battery to see if there was any acid leaking out?
   b Alex's mum said "Let's test the battery to see if it is working OK". Alex wasn't too keen to put it into his radio. So how could he test it? Describe carefully what you would do.
   c Alex didn't want to put the battery into his radio if it was leaking acid. Why not? What problems might it cause?

3 Maria's grandad said it was very dangerous to play with electricity, but Maria said it was safe to use batteries. Her grandad couldn't understand this. How should Maria explain it?

4 Davinder was always buying new batteries for her torch. In the shop she saw that Super-Cell batteries cost 43p each. Kingpower batteries looked the same but only cost 35p each. She wondered which was the best value for money. Kingpower batteries were cheaper, but would they last as long? She decided to buy one of each and carry out some tests. If you were Davinder, what would you do?

Describe carefully, with the help of diagrams, what experiments you would carry out. Say what you would look for, and how you would decide which battery was the best. Be sure to make your tests fair.

© *Borrows, Foster and Richardson 1991*

The greatest sprint race in history

The final of the men's Olympic 100 metre race on September 24th, 1988, was described as the greatest sprint race in history. First came the Canadian, Ben Johnson, who broke both the world and the Olympic record. Second came the American, Carl Lewis, who broke the American record and third came the British runner, Linford Christie, who broke the British and European records. The race was run in less than 10 seconds by the first four runners. (Ben Johnson was later disqualified for taking drugs and therefore did not keep his Olympic gold medal.)

The following table shows the time of each runner at every 10 metres of the race.

DISTANCE IN METRES	START	10	20	30	40	50	60	70	80	90	100
▶ BEN JOHNSON	0.132*	1.95	2.93	3.81	4.69	5.52	6.37	7.22	8.06	8.96	9.79
▶ CARL LEWIS	0.136*	1.97	3.00	3.89	4.81	5.65	6.53	7.37	8.23	9.06	9.92
▶ LINFORD CHRISTIE	0.138*	1.98	3.02	3.92	4.82	5.69	6.55	7.39	8.26	9.11	9.97
▶ CALVIN SMITH	0.176*	2.04	3.06	3.94	4.84	5.70	6.56	7.40	8.27	9.13	9.99

*REACTION TIME TAKEN ELECTRONICALLY FROM FIRING OF STARTER'S PISTOL TO MOMENT WHEN ATHLETE EXPLODES OFF HIS BLOCKS

1
  a What was Ben Johnson's time for the race?
  b Who reached the 50 metre mark at 5.70 seconds?
  c Did the first four runners keep their same positions throughout the race?

2
  a Plot a graph of distance against time for Carl Lewis's race. Plot time along the horizontal axis and distance on the vertical axis.
  b From your graph, how far from the start was Carl Lewis after 5 seconds?
  c The steepness (gradient) of the distance/time graph tells you the speed of the runner at any given time. From your graph, how long did Carl Lewis take to reach his greatest speed?
  d Was Lewis accelerating at the 50 metre mark as stated in the diagram?
  e Did Lewis slow down when he glanced at Johnson at the 90 metre mark?

3
  a What is meant by *reaction time*?
  b Who had the shortest reaction time? What was it?

4 Copy the table below and, using a calculator, complete it for Ben Johnson's race:
  a From this table, where was Ben Johnson when he was running fastest?
  b Use the equation speed = distance/time to find his fastest average speed over 10 metres.

5 Athletes are sometimes paid large sums of money to appear in races or to sponsor sportswear etc. Of course, successful athletes are paid the most. By taking drugs, some athletes, attempt to improve their performance.
  a Do you think athletes should be paid to take part in sport? Give arguments for and against.
  b What type of drugs, if any, should athletes be allowed to take? Give reasons for your answer.

Time (seconds) for each 10 m period										
0–10 m	10–20 m	20–30 m	30–40 m	40–50 m	50–60 m	60–70 m	70–80 m	80–90 m	90–100 m

© Borrows, Foster and Richardson 1991

Mountain bikes

Mountain bikes, also known as "all terrain" bikes, are meant for riding off the roads and over rough ground. The first thing you notice about the bike is the small size of the frame (less distance to fall off!) and the thick knobbly tyres.

The mountain bike frame is made from strong, light, tubular steel or aluminium. The tough wheels have stainless steel spokes. Mountain bikes have strong brakes and many gears (up to 21), to cope with all kinds of terrain, including steep hills. Gears are changed by a lever on the handlebars.

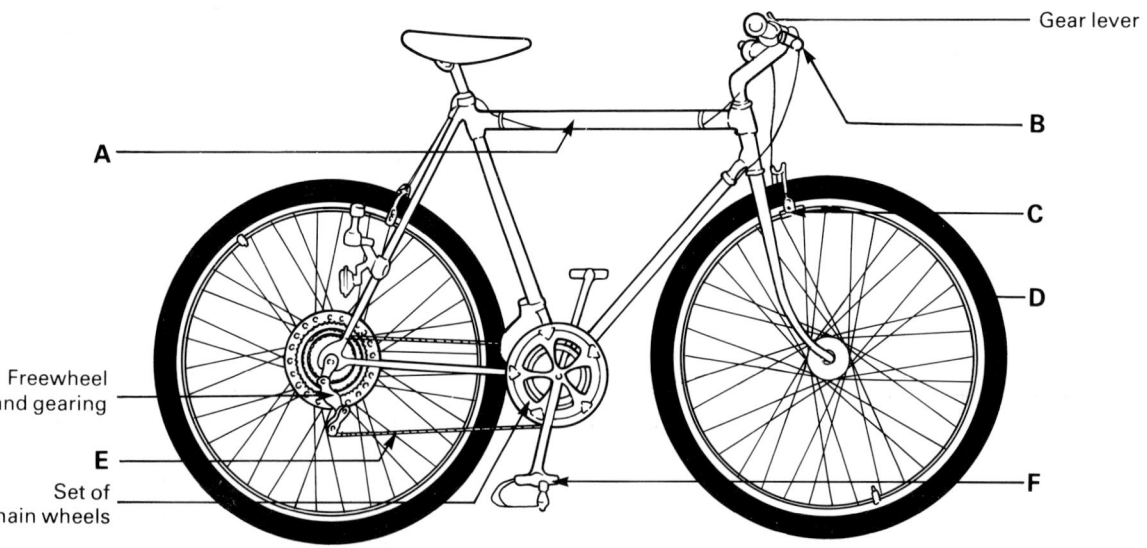

1 Explain why mountain bikes need the following:
   a thick knobbly tyres
   b a small frame
   c strong brakes
   d many gears.

2 a Write out a list of the following bicycle parts: *frame, handlebars, front brakes, front tyre, chain, pedal*. Against each part write the letter used to label it on the line drawing above.
   b On any bicycle, there are a number of levers which enable large forces to be produced by small efforts. For example, the handlebars are a pair of levers. With your hands close to the centre of the handlebars you must exert large forces to turn the front wheel but with your hands far from the centre you can do so with small forces.

   Give *three* more examples of levers to be found on a bicycle and in each case say how they enable the rider's force to be used more effectively.

   c Explain why we don't get more work out of a lever than we put in.
   (*Hint*: Work = force × distance moved by the force).

3 When Sally rides her bike she uses her energy to give the bike movement energy (kinetic energy).
   a Where does Sally get her energy from?
   b Where does the kinetic energy of the bike and rider go as the bike goes up hill?
   c Why are the brake pads on the bike likely to be warm after the bike has been ridden for some time?
   d Explain whether or not the rough ground is likely to be slightly warmer after the bike has travelled across it.

4 Mushtaq says his bike is best at going up hills but Delroy thinks his is better.
   a What do you think they mean by *best*?
   b How could Mushtaq and Delroy set up a fair test to see who is right? Say carefully what they should do, what they should measure and how they could decide who was right.

© *Borrows, Foster and Richardson 1991*

The rock of the Peak District

The Derbyshire Peak District is an area of great natural beauty. The variety of types of rock found there make it attractive. Different types of plants grow on the different rocks.

This map of the Peak District shows the main rocks present on the surface.

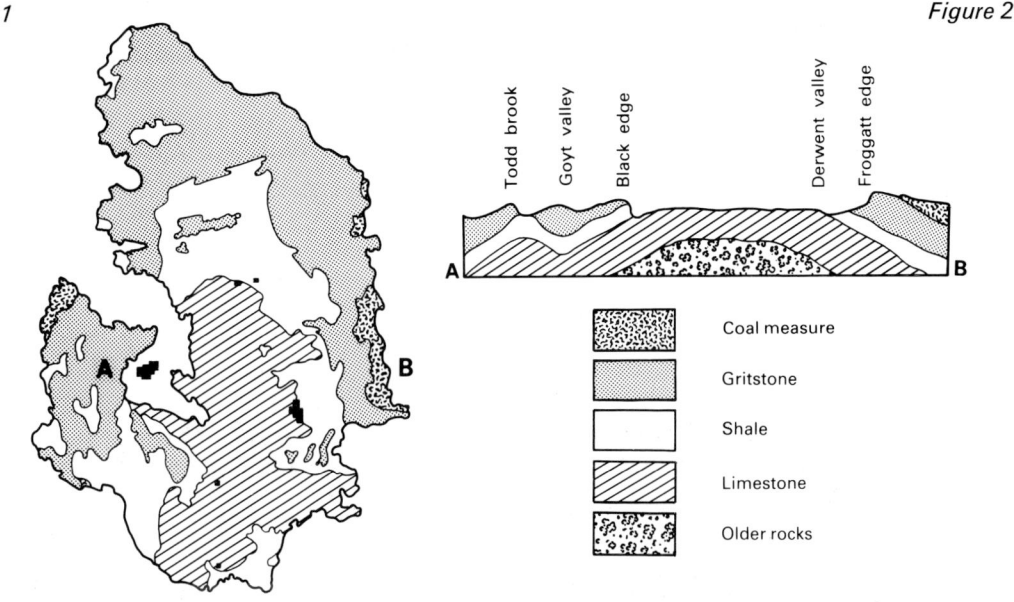

Figure 1

Figure 2

1 a What is the main rock type in the southern part of the Peak District? Suggest why this area is often called the White Peak in guide books.
  b Why do you think the northern part of the Peak District is called the Black Peak in guide books?

Figure 2 shows a section through the Peak District, corresponding to a line from A to B on the map (although not to scale).

2 a The section shows layers of rock. What word is used to describe such layers?
  b In your own words explain how layers of rocks can form.
  c Along this section, which is probably the youngest rock? Why did you choose this rock?
  d Arrange the rocks in a likely order of formation, putting the younger rocks first.

3 Orchids are a type of plant. You can find them growing in the valleys in the southern part of the Peak District, but not in the northern part.
  a Suggest some possible explanations as to why they are found only in the southern part.
  b How would you try to decide which of your explanations was the correct one? What investigations would you carry out?

4 The highest parts along the section are at Black Edge and at Frogatt Edge.
  a What rocks form these high parts?
  b What rocks form the low ground of the Derwent Valley?
  c Which do you think is the harder rock: gritstone or shale? Give a reason for your choice.

5 The rocks of the Peak District have been used for many different purposes.
  a What do you think millstone grit may have been used for? Why would it have been suitable for this purpose?
  b What is coal used for?
  c Limestone is quarried on a very large scale in the Peak District. Find out from books why so much limestone is needed. Make a list of its uses.

6 Some people think it is not a good idea to have quarries and other industrial activities in areas of great natural beauty like the Peak District. Other people think that these activities benefit those who live there. Talk about the advantages and disadvantages with your friends. Then draw up a table like this:

Arguments for	Arguments against

© Borrows, Foster and Richardson 1991

How the Peak District was formed

This extract is from a guidebook to the Derbyshire Peak District, a National Park found at the southern end of the Pennine hills.

> The countryside described in this publication is the nearest thing to a 'walker's paradise' to be found in England.
>
> The rugged and sombre beauty of the millstone-grit country, known as the northern "High" or Black Peak, contrasts strikingly with the somewhat softer loveliness of the dales in the more southerly area called the "Low" or White Peak. Here are beautiful villages which seem almost to have dreamed through the centuries, clear footpaths and ice-cold, sparkling streams tumbling down hillsides patterned by the typical dry-stone walls of Derbyshire.

The Peak District owes much of its beauty to the different rocks found there. These are almost all sedimentary rocks.

About 340 million years ago the area was covered by a tropical sea. This gave rise to the oldest rocks, which are limestones, formed from coral reefs and the shells of sea creatures. Underwater volcanoes erupted occasionally, spreading layers of lava (locally known as "toadstone") over the limestone.

Later, about 310 million years ago, a great river deposited mud and silt over the area. When this in turn was covered by further layers, the weight squeezed the water out of the mud and silt and turned it into the shales we find there today.

Nearer the mouth of the river, heavier particles of sand were deposited and these eventually formed the millstone grit. Plants growing at the swampy edges of the river died, and sometimes became covered with mud. Over millions of years, cut off from the air by heavy layers of rock, these plant remains slowly turned into coal.

---

1 Carefully read the information above. *Underline* the name of every rock which is mentioned. Using a different colour, *underline* each explanation of how the rock was formed.

Then copy this table, and, with the help of your underlinings, fill in the first two columns (leave the last column blank at this stage):

Name of rock	How the rock was formed	Type of rock

2 a What is a fossil?
 b Which of the rocks in the table above are likely to contain fossils? Why?

3 There are three main types of rock found in the earth's crust:

Igneous rock — formed when molten rock from deep underground forces its way up towards the surface of the earth

Sedimentary rock — formed when solid particles settle out as a layer below a body of water

Metamorphic rock — formed from sedimentary rocks by the effects of heat or pressure

Go back to the table you copied in question 1. In the final column fill in igneous, sedimentary or metamorphic as appropriate.

4 Suppose you were given samples of coal, gritstone, limestone and shale. Invent a way of deciding which is the hardest rock, which the second hardest, and so on.
Describe carefully what experiments you would do, what you would look for, and how you would decide your answers.

5 Both limestone and millstone grit are widely used in the Peak District to build houses from.
Make a list of things that you would expect from a good building stone.

© *Borrows, Foster and Richardson 1991*

DISASTERS

Anyone who watches television, or who reads the newspapers, will be only too familiar with these sorts of stories.

THE NIGHT WE NEARLY BLEW AWAY

At least seventeen people were killed yesterday as Britain's worst-ever storm ravaged the country at 100 mph leaving chaos and devastation in its wake.

Last night a Sealink ferry was aground at Folkestone, thousands of homes and buildings were wrecked, cars were crushed and trees uprooted. London was blacked out for six hours in the storm and road and rail networks were paralysed.

WINDS DISRUPT ALASKAN OIL SLICK CLEAN-UP

HIGH WINDS yesterday threatened to bring ecological disaster to the once pristine waters of Prince William Sound, Alaska, scene of America's biggest oil spill.

Efforts to mop up the 240,000 barrels of heavy Alaskan crude were disrupted by near gale-force winds and seven-foot waves. The oil slick, now said to be covering 100 square miles, was driven beyond protective booms towards the surrounding islands and inlets teeming with fish, birds and animals.

Del Ruiz rumbles

Colombia's 17,500ft Del Ruiz volcano spewed ash and steam yesterday, and several villages were evacuated. About 23,000 people were killed in the volcano's last big eruption in 1985, many buried alive in the town of Armero.

There are many sorts of disasters. Here are some examples:

Train crash   Floods   Earthquake   War

Volcano   Oil spill   Drought   Hurricane

1 Some of these disasters are definitely due to the activities of people. Some are due to the weather. Some are due to events deep underneath the earth's crust.
  a Decide whether the cause of each of the eight disasters listed above is people, weather, or the earth. Draw up a suitable table to record your decisions.
  b Which of the disasters listed could be prevented?

2 Read the account of the hurricane in Britain.
  a How is wind speed measured?
  b What actually is wind?
  c Under what conditions of air pressure are you likely to get the highest wind speeds?
  d Will the hurricane cause a permanent change in the landscape? Explain your answer.

3 a Explain in your own words what happens in a volcanic eruption. Draw a diagram to illustrate your answer.
  b Will a volcanic eruption cause a permanent change in the landscape?
  c What type of rock is formed from a volcano: sedimentary, igneous or metamorphic?
  d What happens to a volcano when it is no longer active? Does the mound of lava stay there for ever?
  e Astronauts on the Apollo programme brought many rock samples back from the moon. All the samples were igneous rock. Why was there no sedimentary rock?

4 The oil spill in Alaska caused a lot of damage to wildlife. Many sea birds were covered in oil.
  a Scientists try to remove the oil with a solvent. How does a solvent remove oil?
  b Suppose you were a scientist trying to find the best solvent to use. What sort of things would it be important to think about when choosing a solvent?
  c Plan an investigation to find the best solvent to use. Say what equipment you would use, what you would do, and how you would work out your results.

5 Some people don't think it is right to have oil pipelines in areas of great beauty like Alaska, especially with the risks to wildlife. Other people argue that we need the oil.
What do you think? Write a letter to the newspaper that published this story.

© *Borrows, Foster and Richardson 1991*

Radioactivity 2

When unstable nuclei split up giving out radiation, they change into new nuclei. In this way, one element may change into another. The process is called *radioactive decay*. Because radioactive decay happens by chance, we cannot say when a particular nucleus will split up, but given a great number of nuclei, we can say that, on average, after a certain time, half the nuclei will split up, or decay. The time taken for half of a sample of radioactive atoms to decay is called the half-life.

> **Radon is a natural radioactive gas, believed to be responsible for 2500 lung cancers every year.**
>
> **It is odourless and seeps upwards from rocks containing uranium. If radon is detected then homes can have floors sealed and ventilation installed. Some 60,000 houses are believed to be affected by radon.**

For example, one kind or *isotope* of radon (radon-222) has a half-life of four days. It decays into another element, polonium, which being radioactive itself decays into another, and so on.

---

1 Imagine that you had a tube containing 32 g of the radioactive gas radon-222. After four days you would only have 16 g; four days later 8 g, and so on.

  a Plot a graph of mass of radon-222 against time. Make the time axis horizontal and the mass axis vertical. Start with 32 g at time zero. Plot the mass the radon would have after every four days, for 20 days.

  b According to your graph, how many grammes of radon would you have after 20 days?

  c If you kept the tube for much longer (1000 days or more, say) do you think that you would ever have *no* radon left? Explain.

  d If radon decays with a half-life of four days, why is there a permanent radon problem for people living in certain districts?

  e As the radon in your tube decays, does the tube get appreciably lighter? Explain.

© Borrows, Foster and Richardson 1991

Radioactivity 1

Something is radioactive if it is made up of atoms which are unstable. The nuclei of these atoms split up, giving out *ionising* radiation which can be harmful. This *nuclear* radiation can be detected with a *Geiger counter*.

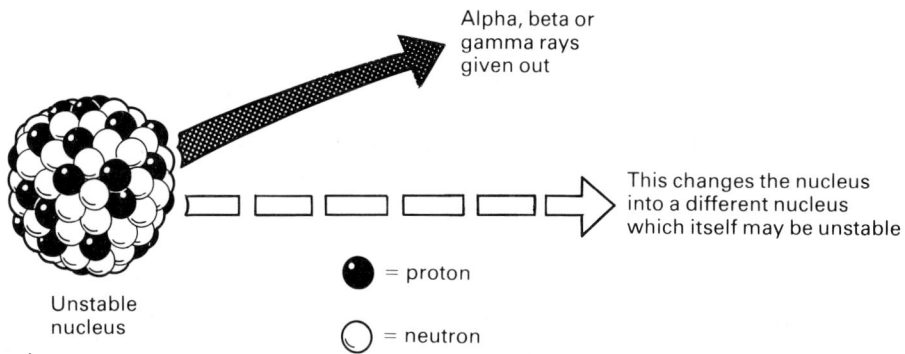

We can be exposed to nuclear radiation from both natural and man-made sources. Because of radioactive materials in the ground, in objects around us and in the air, we are exposed to *background* radiation all the time. Some rocks contain more radioactive material than others. For example, granite is normally radioactive. So if you live in an area where there is a lot of granite, you are likely to be exposed to a higher level of background radiation than would otherwise be the case.

Artificial sources of radioactivity include nuclear power stations, hospital radiation treatment machines and even things in the home like smoke detectors and some luminous watch dials. Unless there is a nuclear war or an accident, for most people, the dose of radiation received from natural sources will be far greater than that received from artificial sources.

---

1 a State *two* things which the nuclei of *radioactive* atoms do.

b Name a device used for detecting nuclear radiation.

c What do we call radiation from natural materials around us?

d Mention a place near your home where granite is to be found (often in the street).

e What happened at Hiroshima in Japan on August 6th, 1945?

f What happened at Chernobyl in the USSR on April 26th 1986?

© *Borrows, Foster and Richardson 1991*

Radiation treatment

The word *radiation* is used to describe the carrying of energy by rays through space. A hot object gives out infrared or heat radiation. A substance which is radioactive (a radio-isotope) gives out alpha, beta or gamma radiation. This *nuclear* radiation comes from the unstable nuclei of certain atoms. Gamma rays are the most highly penetrating form of nuclear radiation. Like X-rays, they can travel through the human body. Gamma rays are not easily stopped; they can travel through as much as 5 cm of lead.

CANCER CURE BUNGLE KILLS PATIENT

A patient was cured of cancer but died as a result of a radiation overdose, an inquest heard yesterday.

The patient was one of 153 cancer patients who suffered a radiation overdose because of a wrong setting on a Telecobalt machine. It happened because the medical physicist got his sums wrong when setting the machine.

The coroner recorded a verdict of *"misadventure aggravated by lack of care."*

Nuclear radiation can be put to many practical uses, apart from radiation treatment. The most well known uses are nuclear power stations and nuclear weapons. But there are very many other uses. For example, the ordinary household smoke detector contains a small quantity of radioactive material. Satellites and space probes often carry radioactive material to act as a power source. Engineers use radioisotopes to locate leaks in underground pipes; research chemists use radioisotopes to follow chemical reactions. All of these uses carry some risk, because the radiation, if allowed to escape, can destroy healthy human cells in the same way it destroys cancerous cells during radiation treatment.

It may be, in some cases, that the risk to a person's life of using radioactivity can outweigh the benefits. One thing is certain, though. We can never fully escape from nuclear radiation, as we receive a low background dose, all the time, from naturally occurring radioisotopes in the air around us and in the rocks beneath our feet.

---

1 List *three* factors which govern the amount of radiation dose received from a radioisotope. *Hint*: what would affect the amount of heat you receive when warming yourself in front of a two-bar radiant electric fire?

2 a What is the name of the radiation treatment machine used in the hospital and mentioned in the press cutting?

  b From the name of the machine, which radioactive element do you think it uses?

3 The radiation source referred to in the press cutting gives out gamma rays which can be passed into the patient's body from different directions.

  a How does the radiation physicist ensure that he or she does not become exposed to the gamma rays?

  b How might radiation be directed into a patient's body, in order to knock out cancerous tissue, without harming healthy tissue? Sketch your answer.

4 The article above is from the *Daily Mirror*. Write a letter to the editor of the *Daily Mirror* giving your views about the accident described in the newspaper cutting. Point out some of the benefits which nuclear radiation can give to people and say how you think the risks can be reduced.

© Borrows, Foster and Richardson 1991

1
 a What indicators have you used in school?
 b Were they ready made, or did you make your own? If so, how?
 c What colour changes did they undergo with acids and alkalis?
 d Suppose you are given some blackcurrant juice. How would you test it to see if it acts as an indicator? Describe what you would do, what you would use, and what you would look for.

2 Many plants and animals use acids or alkalis as a way of defending themselves against attack, or as a method of attacking others. Read this article in *The Guardian*.

> **Stinging defence of the nettle**
>
> Until modern times nettles were commonly collected, and sometimes cultivated, for use as a food. Nettle leaves are rich in iron and other nutrients, and are believed to help relieve such ailments as rheumatism, sciatica, and high blood pressure. The young shoots are the best to eat, and although quite bland as a plain vegetable, they make a delicious soup. The formic acid which causes the sting is destroyed by cooking.

 a If you get stung by an ant, it injects a tiny amount of formic acid into you. You might be able to relieve the pain by wiping the area with an alkali such as sodium bicarbonate. Explain why this would work.
 b An old book suggests that a dab of vinegar is an effective way of easing the pain of a wasp sting. What do you think is present in the sting of a wasp?
 c The same book suggests a different remedy for bee stings: dab the sting with a dilute solution of ammonia, or just rub it with wet soap. Why do you think either ammonia or wet soap can be used for bee stings?
 d One book suggests that if you get stung by a nettle, wiping the area with an alkali does *not* work. Does that fit in with what is suggested in *The Guardian* letter? Carefully explain your answer.

3 Bacteria in your mouth will turn sugar into acid.
 a Where does the sugar in your mouth come from?
 b What effect do you think the acid will have on your teeth?
 c Cleaning your teeth with toothpaste might just wash away the acid, or it might neutralise the acid. If it was going to neutralise the acid, what sort of chemical would have to be present in the toothpaste?
 d How would you try to find out whether your toothpaste was actually neutralising the acid? Describe carefully what experiments you would do, how you would do them, and what you would look out for.
 e Some people say that the acid in fizzy drinks attacks your teeth. Plan an investigation to find out whether your favourite fizzy drink causes any damage to teeth. Describe what you would do, how you would do it, how you would make your tests fair, and how you would decide whether the drink really does damage your teeth.

4 Read this story from the *Daily Mirror*.

> **KISS 'N' TELL LIPSTICK**
>
> A TELLTALE lipstick which gives the game away when a girl fancies a bloke has been invented by some cosmetics experts.
>
> The lipstick, now on sale on the Continent, turns a deep shade of red when the wearer is turned on.
>
> A chemical in the lipstick reacts with acidity in the skin which increases with sexual excitement.
>
> But if a girl's lipstick stays pale, chaps, it means you leave her cold. The kiss 'n' tell lipstick, developed in Holland, is likely to be launched in Britain soon.
>
> It is guaranteed kiss-proof and the chemical effect lasts for 12 hours.

 a How could you test to see if your perspiration (or sweat) is acidic?
 b If the lipstick is going to change colour in this way, what sort of chemical must be present in the lipstick?
 c What do you think might happen to the deep red lipstick if some toothpaste got onto it? Explain your answer.

© Borrows, Foster and Richardson 1991

Acids, alkalis and indicators all around us

Acids are all around us. The word acid just means "sour": for example, sour milk contains lactic acid. The sharp taste of various fruits is due to different acids. Oranges and lemons contain citric acid; apples contain malic acid; grapes contain tartaric acid; rhubarb contains oxalic acid. Many foods and drinks also contain acids.

A substance that is capable of removing the sharp taste of an acid is called an alkali. Alkalis are not so common in foods, but "bicarb", often used in cooking, is an alkali (its chemical name is sodium bicarbonate or sodium hydrogencarbonate). We often use alkalis for cleaning purposes around the home. Ammonia is an alkali, as are soaps and detergents.

When an alkali removes the sharp taste of an acid we say the acid is neutralised. Your stomach contains acid (hydrochloric acid) and indigestion is caused by too much acid. It can be cured by neutralising some of it with an alkali, such as milk of magnesia.

Obviously, it would be dangerous to taste things to see if they have the sharp taste of an acid, so we usually use indicators. Indicators will go different colours in acids and alkalis. Coloured materials from many plants act as indicators – for example, rose petals, red cabbage, beetroot, and so on.

© Borrows, Foster and Richardson 1991

1 **a** The advertisement says we don't drive cars *in a vacuum*. What do we drive cars in?
   b Give *one* reason why cars would not work in a vacuum.

2 The advertisement mentions the *names* of four chemicals. One of these is nitric acid. Find the others, and then copy and complete this table:

Name of chemical	Is it an element or a compound?
Nitric acid	

3 **a** Explain why the advertisement talks about "A few <u>billion</u> <u>little</u> reasons". Be sure to comment on both of the underlined words.
   b In what way(s) is the drawing *not* a realistic representation of molecules in the air?

4 **a** You probably know the names of the main gases present in air. What are they? What percentage of each is there in normal air?
   b Air is one example of a mixture that occurs naturally. Give *two* more examples.

5 There are seven different chemicals (1, 2, ... 7) represented in the drawings in the advertisement. These are shown in the first two columns of the table below.
Copy the table carefully, and complete it.

6 It would be rather boring having to do these drawings all the time, so chemists often use a sort of shorthand. A chemical symbol consists of one or two letters. These are the symbols for the atoms shown in the advertisement:

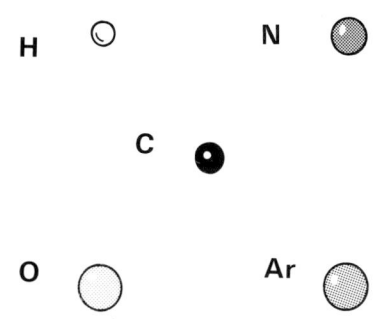

Chemical number 1 would be written as CO_2

Chemical number 7 would be written as N_2

   a How would each of chemicals 2 to 6 be written using chemical symbols?
   b Can you now give the *names* of each of the chemicals 1, 2, 3, 4, 5, 6 and 7?
   c For each of the chemicals you have just named, find out and write a little about its chemistry.

Chemical	Drawing	Is it an atom or a molecule?	Is it an element or a compound?
1			
2			
3			
4			
5			
6			
7			

© Borrows, Foster and Richardson 1991

Molecules in the air

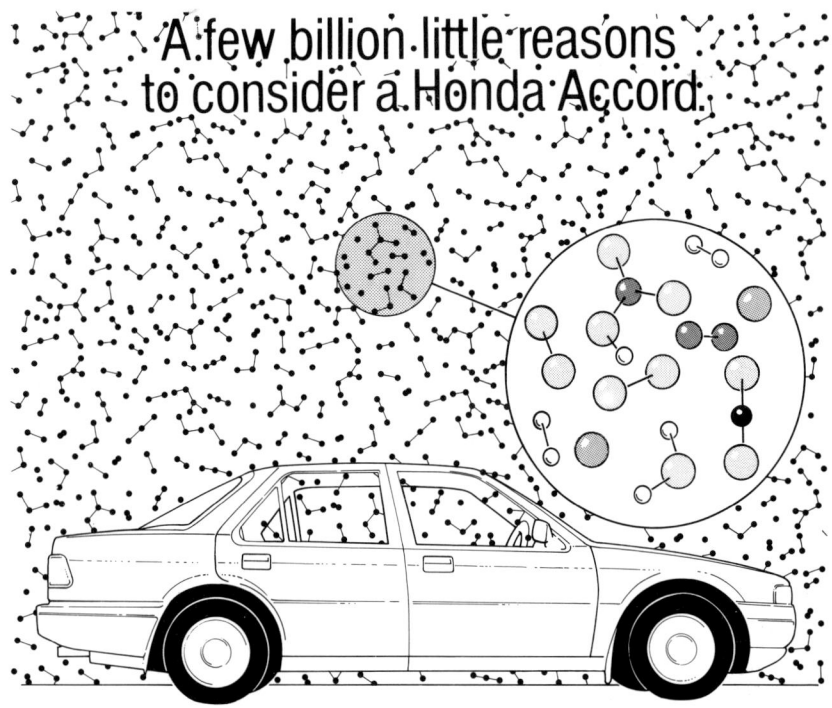

A few billion little reasons to consider a Honda Accord.

You don't drive a car in a vacuum. It, and you, are surrounded. By nitrogen, by oxygen, by argon, by rare compounds with strange names. In short, by that molecular soup we call air.

If that sounds like a statement of the obvious, then what follows is not. Air affects the performance of car and driver in a host of unexpected ways. Oxygen plays a vital role in the engine. Airborne corrosive agents like nitric acid can play havoc with your paintwork.

This is part of an advertisement for Honda cars. (The advertisement has been slightly modified, because the original was in colour). The advertiser is trying to show that air is a complicated mixture of elements and compounds, of atoms and molecules, which can affect cars in many ways.

An *element* cannot be split into anything simpler. It is made up of just one sort of atom,

For example or

Sometimes, these atoms may go around by themselves,

but more commonly they join together in pairs,

Two or more atoms joined together are called *molecules*. A *compound* is composed of two or more different sorts of atoms joined together to form molecules.

For example,  or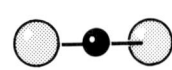

turn

© *Borrows, Foster and Richardson 1991*

After a few days, she looked at her experiment. These were some of her results:

Material used	Had the crystals gone pink?
None (tube X)	Yes
Plastic carrier bag	No
Silica gel packet	Yes

1 a Look up the word *desiccant* in a dictionary. What does it mean?
  b Why do you think the label says "Do not eat"?

2 a Marie had seen some paper in her science lessons that changed from blue to pink when water was added to it. You probably have as well. What is it called?
  b When Marie warmed the white crystals *she saw some steamy fumes, and on the cool part of the test tube she saw drops of clear liquid.* She thought this might be water. How could she test the liquid to see if it really was water?
  Describe what she should do and what she should look out for.

3 a Why did Marie set up tube X?
  b Do you think the plastic from the carrier bag let moisture through?
  c Do you think the material from the silica gel packet let moisture through?
  d What do you think might happen with some of the other materials she used? Give a reason for your answer.

4 The silica gel packet was to stop any metal parts in her camera going rusty in its box. For iron or steel to go rusty you need both water and oxygen (from the air). Iron will not go rusty with pure water by itself.
  a What experiment would you do to show that oxygen (or air) is also necessary for iron to go rusty?
  b Motorists usually say their cars go rusty more quickly in winter, and blame it on the salt on the roads. How could you show that salt makes things go rusty more quickly?
  Describe carefully the experiments you would do. Say what you would use, what you would look for, and how you would decide if salt does make a difference.

5 We use many ways of stopping things from going rusty, apart from little packets of silica gel. We paint things, we chromium plate them, we cover them with grease...
Look around your home and your neighbourhood. Make a list of the different things made from iron or steel, and for each one write down what has been done to stop it from going rusty.

© Borrows, Foster and Richardson 1991

RUSTING

Marie was given a new camera. When she opened the box, she found a small packet inside, next to the camera. Inside the packet were some white crystals, together with a few blue ones.

This is what the packet looked like:

Marie decided to do some experiments with the silica gel crystals. She put a few of them in a test tube, and added a few drops of water. The white crystals didn't seem to do anything much, but the blue ones went pink.

Marie then took some more of the white crystals, and warmed them gently in a clean dry test tube. She saw some steamy fumes, and on the cool parts of the test tube she saw drops of a clear liquid. She thought this might be water.

Marie decided that the purpose of the silica gel crystals was to soak up any moisture, so that any metal parts of her camera did not go rusty. But she was puzzled about the packet that the crystals were in. It wasn't paper, but it didn't seem to be plastic either. It had to let moisture through, but it mustn't go soggy. She decided to try another experiment.

She got six clean dry test tubes. Into each one she put a few of the blue crystals. Then she covered the top of each test tube with different materials, which she held in place with a rubber band. As well as a piece of the packet for the silica gel, she used a bit of a plastic carrier bag, a bit cut from a crisp packet, cling flim, and so on. One test tube (tube X) didn't have anything on the top. Then she stood all the test tubes in a big box with a lid. Also in the box, she put a beaker of water. This is what it looked like:

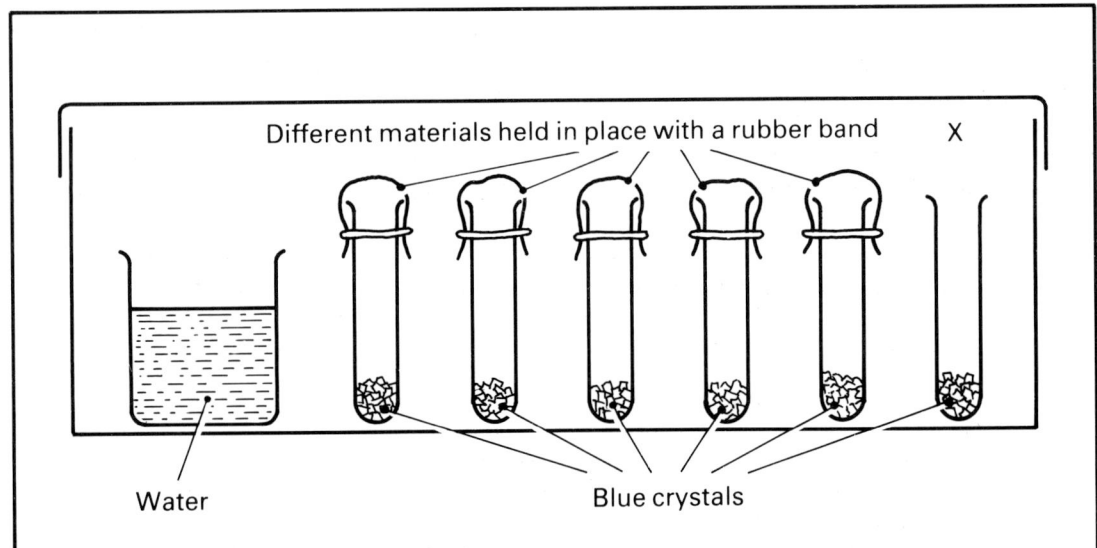

© Borrows, Foster and Richardson 1991

Acid rain in Epping Forest

Acid test for trees

TREES in southern England – including Epping Forest – are sick and dying because of air pollution, according to environmental group Greenpeace.

Scientist Andrew Tickle made a survey for the group of more than 1,000 yew, beech and oak trees. He found that three quarters of yew trees were damaged with one-tenth beyond hope of recovery.

More than half the oak trees were damaged with seven per cent dying and over a third of beech trees were damaged with three per cent dying.

Mr Tickle says the evidence is that the widespread damage cannot be explained by natural causes, and points out that trees next to trunk roads and motorways were particularly poor.

He blames soil disturbance, salt damage and exhaust from vehicles for the problem.

Greenpeace has been campaigning to get car manufacturers to fit vehicles with converters to cut out 90 per cent of harmful gases. But although the technology has been known for a decade, converters are not available in Britain.

When petrol is burnt in a car engine it forms carbon dioxide and water. We say the fuel is *oxidised*. If it doesn't burn properly, you might get carbon monoxide, which is poisonous. When petrol burns you will get also small amounts of sulphur dioxide, from impurities in the petrol. In the very hot conditions of a car engine, nitrogen and oxygen from the air may join together to form nitrogen oxides. Sulphur dioxide and nitrogen oxides dissolve in rain water to make acid rain.

Carbon monoxide and nitrogen oxides (but *not* sulphur dioxide) can be removed by using converters (more properly, "catalytic converters"). The carbon monoxide would be *oxidised* to carbon dioxide. The nitrogen oxides would lose their oxygen and be *reduced* to nitrogen. The catalyst itself, in the converter, is not changed (although it may slowly become poisoned). The catalyst just speeds up certain desirable chemical changes, and makes them happen before the exhaust gases leave the car. Thus the car produces less pollution.

---

1 Read the article carefully.
  a What evidence is there, in the article, that cars are causing damage to the trees of Epping Forest?
  b Although car exhausts get most of the blame in this article, other possible causes are suggested as well. What are they?
  c According to the article, Greenpeace wants car manufacturers to fit a converter to the exhaust system. What would this do?

2 Suppose you had just read the above article in the newspaper. Write a letter to the editor of the paper, giving your views on the problem.

3 What do you understand by the term *catalyst*? Look the word up in a book if you have not met it before.

4 Read carefully the information in the passages. Then copy out and complete this table:

Starting material	End product	Where it happens	Type of reaction
Hydrocarbon fuel	Water & carbon dioxide		Oxidation
Carbon monoxide		Converter	
Nitrogen oxides			

© *Borrows, Foster and Richardson 1991*

1
 a Roughly speaking, when do you think the church was built?
 b For how long, therefore, has it been exposed to the polluted London air?
 c The church is mainly built from ragstone. Where was this quarried?

2
 a What fossil fuels are mentioned in the passage?
 b What is meant by a fossil fuel?
 c Give the name of another fossil fuel, not mentioned here.

3 Read the information in the passage and *underline* the name of each pollutant. Then, using a pen or pencil of a different colour, *underline* how the pollutant is formed. Finally, using a third colour, *underline* whether it will affect stonework or not.

Now copy and complete the following table:

Pollutant	How it is formed	Does it affect stonework?

4 Ragstone is a type of sandstone. It is a sedimentary rock which consists of grains of sand stuck together with a natural cement of calcium carbonate.
 a What is meant by a *sedimentary rock*?
 b If you put a piece of ragstone into a test tube of acid, you see bubbles of gas. Predict what gas this is likely to be.
 c How could you test the gas to see if you were right?
 d However much acid is used, some of the ragstone remains undissolved. How would you separate these remains from the acid?
 e When examined carefully, these undissolved remains look just like grains of sand. What effect, if any, do you think acid has on sand?
 f What effect, if any, do you think acid has on the calcium carbonate present in ragstone?
 g Explain why acid rain is making the stone of this church crumble away.

5 If you were going to build a church now, you would want to choose a building material that would not crumble away in a hundred years' time. You might consider bricks, or concrete, or granite, or other materials. How would you investigate whether or not any of these was better at resisting attack by acid rain than ragstone is? Describe carefully any experiments you would do, how you would make your tests fair, what you would look for, and how you would decide what was the best material to use.

Do you think acid rain is the only thing you would need to investigate, or should you consider other problems as well?

© *Borrows, Foster and Richardson 1991*

Crumbling church

This is part of a leaflet appealing for money to repair a church in the suburbs of London.

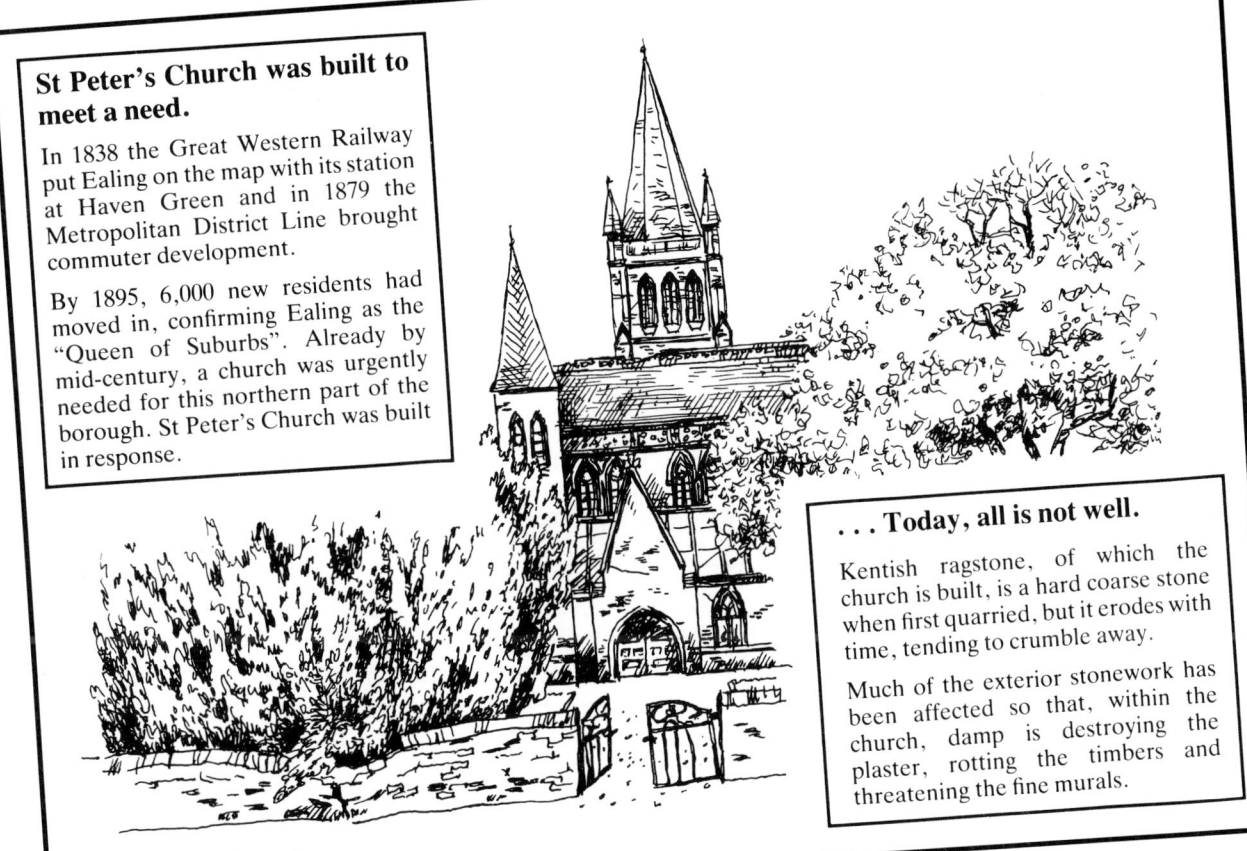

St Peter's Church was built to meet a need.

In 1838 the Great Western Railway put Ealing on the map with its station at Haven Green and in 1879 the Metropolitan District Line brought commuter development.

By 1895, 6,000 new residents had moved in, confirming Ealing as the "Queen of Suburbs". Already by mid-century, a church was urgently needed for this northern part of the borough. St Peter's Church was built in response.

... Today, all is not well.

Kentish ragstone, of which the church is built, is a hard coarse stone when first quarried, but it erodes with time, tending to crumble away.

Much of the exterior stonework has been affected so that, within the church, damp is destroying the plaster, rotting the timbers and threatening the fine murals.

Much of the damage to the stone has been caused by the polluted London air. There are a number of causes of air pollution. Fossil fuels, such as coal and oil, are mainly composed of carbon and hydrogen. If they burn properly, carbon dioxide and water will form. These are not usually regarded as pollutants. But if the air supply is not good enough, carbon monoxide or carbon might form. Carbon monoxide would not damage the stone, although it is poisonous. Carbon, more usually known as soot, would blacken the stonework.

Most fossil fuels contain small amounts of sulphur, and so would form some sulphur dioxide when they burn. This dissolves in rainwater to produce an acid which will damage some building stones. The amount of sulphur dioxide and carbon is much *less* now in London air than it was forty or a hundred years ago. This is because although there are more cars, there are far fewer coal fires. Domestic coal fires used to cause a lot of the pollution.

Cars also cause another sort of pollution – nitrogen oxides. In a car engine, a spark passes through a mixture of air and petrol. The spark is meant to ignite the petrol, but it also causes some of the nitrogen and oxygen to combine, forming nitrogen oxides. These in turn dissolve in rain water to give an acid. About one third of the acidity in rain water is due to nitrogen oxides.

Cars that use leaded petrol will also produce lead oxide as a pollutant. Although this is poisonous it will not damage the church.

turn

© Borrows, Foster and Richardson 1991

PIPELINE

There are many places in Britain where you might spot a sign like this one:

Pipelines carrying not only gas but also oil and other chemicals criss-cross the countryside. They are usually buried out of view, with only markers such as this to show where the are.

The second picture shows the construction of an oil pipeline in 1985 from an oil refinery at Fawley (near Southampton) to storage tanks near Birmingham.

Oil and gas are often found in similar types of rock, sometimes both occurring together.

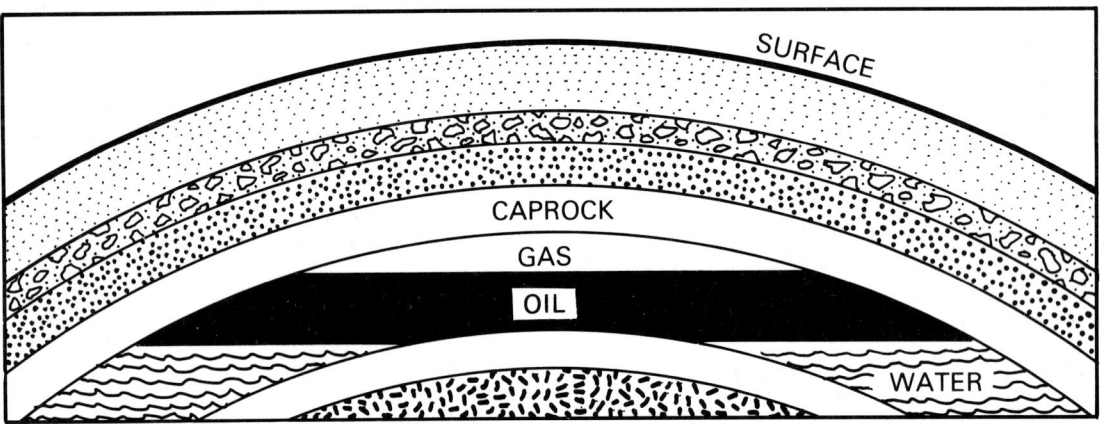

1 a Why is it necessary to have gas pipelines?
  b Both oil and gas are fuels. What is meant by a fuel?
  c In fact, oil and gas are *fossil* fuels. How were they formed?
  d As well as being fuels, both oil and gas are important raw materials for the chemical industry. What is meant by the term *raw material*?
  e What is the purpose of an oil refinery, such as that at Fawley?

2 a What word is used to describe layers of rock, as shown in the diagram?
  b What is meant by the *caprock*?
  c The caprock is said to be "impervious" or "non-porous". What does this mean?
  d Why does the oil or gas get trapped in the porous rock?
  e Why is the layer of gas above the layer of oil, and the layer of oil above the layer of water?
  f How do geologists attempt to find where oil or gas may be trapped?

3 Many people are worried that if we continue to use oil and gas at the present rate, we may run out before very long.
  a Why would this be a problem?
  b Write a letter to your local newspaper saying what you think we should do, so that we don't run out of oil or gas.

© *Borrows, Foster and Richardson 1991*

FIZZY DRINKS

Carbonated ("fizzy") drinks are very popular. They include lemonade (and other ... ades), cola drinks, and soda water as well as water from natural springs. This is part of the label from a bottle of Spring Water.

※ **SPRING** ※

Carbonated Natural Mineral Water

SPARKLING

2 LITRE e

BOTTLED AT SOURCE

SERVE CHILLED

This refreshing crystal clear water emerges from its deep natural underground source which is situated 1000 feet up in the Derbyshire Peak District.

Composition in accordance with the results of the officially recognised analysis of 9th September 1985.

All carbonated drinks are solutions. Carbon dioxide is dissolved in the liquid, under pressure. Gradually, the carbon dioxide comes out of solution. Usually, there will be other things dissolved as well – flavourings of various sorts, sweeteners, preservatives, and so on. Natural spring waters will often have substances which were dissolved from some of the rocks through which the water flowed.

1 a You often hear a "Psssshhhh..." sound when you open a bottle or can of a carbonated drink. What do you think causes this sound?
  b If you shake up the bottle or can, the contents all squirt out when you open it. Why do you think this happens?
  c The label above says *Serve chilled*. Apart from being a less refreshing drink, what will happen if the drink is warmed up?

2 Carbonated drinks are all solutions.
  a What is the solvent in these drinks?
  b Most carbonated drinks contain several solutes: which solute is present in all of them?
  c Explain what the words *solvent* and *solute* mean.

3 The composition of Spring Water is not given on the label. The Derbyshire Peak District is an area with lots of limestone rocks. The limestone could dissolve to give calcium salts in solution.
  a How could you try to find out if there are any dissolved solids in Spring Water? Describe what you would do, and what you would look for.
  b You might try to prove that calcium was present by doing a "flame test". If you have done this test in the laboratory before, describe what you would do, and what you would look for.
  If you have not yet done a flame test, try and find out from a book what is involved.

4 Spring Water is described as *crystal clear*, so there can't be any specks of solids floating in it. Any such solids have been removed by natural filters.
  a Explain what *filtering* is.
  b What are the natural filters that make Spring Water so clear?

5 Suppose you had a full bottle of Spring Water, and you wanted to measure how much carbon dioxide there was dissolved in it. Invent a way of doing this, using equipment which is readily available to you.
In pencil, draw a labelled diagram to show what you would use. Explain carefully how you would use it.

6 Although Spring Water does not do so, most cans and bottles of carbonated drinks give a detailed list of the contents. Get together with a group of friends, and carry out a survey to find out what is in different brands of carbonated drinks. Present your results in such a way that it is easy to compare different drinks. Try to identify which things are present as preservatives, which as sweeteners, and so on.

© *Borrows, Foster and Richardson 1991*

LEMONADE BOTTLE

The picture shows an almost empty bottle of lemonade. Lemonade is a solution. It contains various flavourings dissolved in water. Carbon dioxide also dissolves in the water, but gradually escapes, especially if the top is left off, or if the lemonade is left in a warm place. Sugar and most other solids become *more* soluble in water as the temperature gets higher. Carbon dioxide and most other gases get *less* soluble in water as the temperature gets higher.

3 a The liquid present in the bottle of lemonade is obviously lemonade, but what is the gas?
  b How would you try to prove to somebody that you were right about what the gas is?

4 a Give the name of *one* material commonly used to make the bottles for putting lemonade in.
  b Give at least *two* reasons why this is quite a good material to make lemonade bottles from.
  c What problems may be caused by using this material for lemonade bottles?
  d Suggest an alternative material for making lemonade bottles which does not have these problems.

5 The bottle of lemonade has a screw cap. Sometimes screw caps are made of plastic, sometimes of metal.
  a Everyone can recognise whether a cap is plastic or metal just by looking at it and feeling it.
    What properties help you to say "This is metal" or "This is plastic"?
  b If a cap is made of metal, it could be aluminium or steel. How would you decide which it was?

6 Why does a glass of lemonade go "flat" more quickly on a warm day than a cold day?

7 If you have a freshly opened bottle or can of lemonade (or any other fizzy drink), you can try this investigation:
Pour some lemonade into a glass. Add a few grains of salt. What do you observe? If you add more salt, does the same thing happen?
What happens if you add other things instead of salt – such as sugar, or potato crisps? Write about your investigation, saying what you did and what you observed. What explanation can you suggest for what is happening? How would you try to prove that your explanation was correct?

1 a Use a pencil to draw a neat picture of the bottle of lemonade.
  b Label your drawing to show clearly a solid, a liquid, and a gas.
  c In your own words, and using the bottle of lemonade as an example if you want to, explain the differences between solids, liquids and gases.

2 a What equipment would you use to measure the volume of lemonade left in the bottle?
  b How could you measure the volume of gas in the bottle?

© Borrows, Foster and Richardson 1991

Soil test kit

It is important to be able to measure how strongly acid or alkaline something is. We use the pH scale to do this. At school, you have probably used a pH scale something like this one. The pH of a few things have been marked on it.

```
Strong          Weak      Neutral    Weak          Strong
acids           acids                alkalis       alkalis

 1    2    3    4    5    6    7    8    9   10   11   12   13   14
 ↑                                       ↑                         ↑
Car                                     Soap                     Drain
battery                                                          cleaner
```

1 a What did you use to test pH at school?
 b Suppose you were trying to find the pH of orange juice at school, what would you do?

2 a How would you describe something that has a pH = 7?
 b What is the pH of soap?
 c Copy the scale. Then using arrows, mark on it roughly where you would expect the pH of some other things to be. You may have tested some things at school, or you may be able to guess some. What about vinegar, tap water, cola drinks, tooth paste, lemon juice, milk of magnesia? Add any more things you know about.

The extract opposite is from a set of instructions for the Rapitest Soil Test Kit. This kit allows gardeners to test the pH of their soil (and to test for other things in the soil). Read the information carefully.

3 a Why is it useful for gardeners to know the pH of their soil?
 b The pH scale which was supplied with the kit was *not* like the one shown above. It only went from pH 4.5 to pH 7.5, instead of from pH 1 to pH 14. Why do you think this was?
 c If a gardener finds that the soil is too acidic, what can he or she do about it?

4 a The instructions tell you to take soil samples from different parts of the garden, and test them separately, rather than mixing them together. Why do you think that this is necessary?
 b Why do the instructions suggest testing the same sample of soil several times?
 c Why do you think it is necessary to filter the solution before checking the colour of it against the pH chart?

RAPITEST SOIL TEST KIT

Take the guesswork out of gardening!

Test for pH
You need to control how acid or alkaline your soil is because plants have such different pH needs.

Your first job should be to make sure that the pH – the alkalinity/acidity level of your soil is correct for each of your plants. Test for pH in different areas – vegetables, fruit, flowers, shrubs, lawn – then refer to our special list of plant pH needs. You can then either choose plants to suit your soil or alter the pH of the soil to suit the plant.

Preparing samples of soil
Take soil samples from a depth of about 4 inches. Place in a clean container. Break up the sample using a spoon and remove any small stones and unwanted organic matter. Mix the sample thoroughly and allow it to dry naturally.

It's preferable to make individual tests on several samples of soil from different parts of the garden rather than to mix several samples together.

For greater accuracy make several tests on the same sample and average results.

Doing the tests
Add the test solution to the 2ml mark for *all* tests. Shake the soil and solution together for 30 seconds. Filter the mixture into a test tube.

Immediately compare the colour of the solution with the pH reading chart.

© Borrows, Foster and Richardson 1991

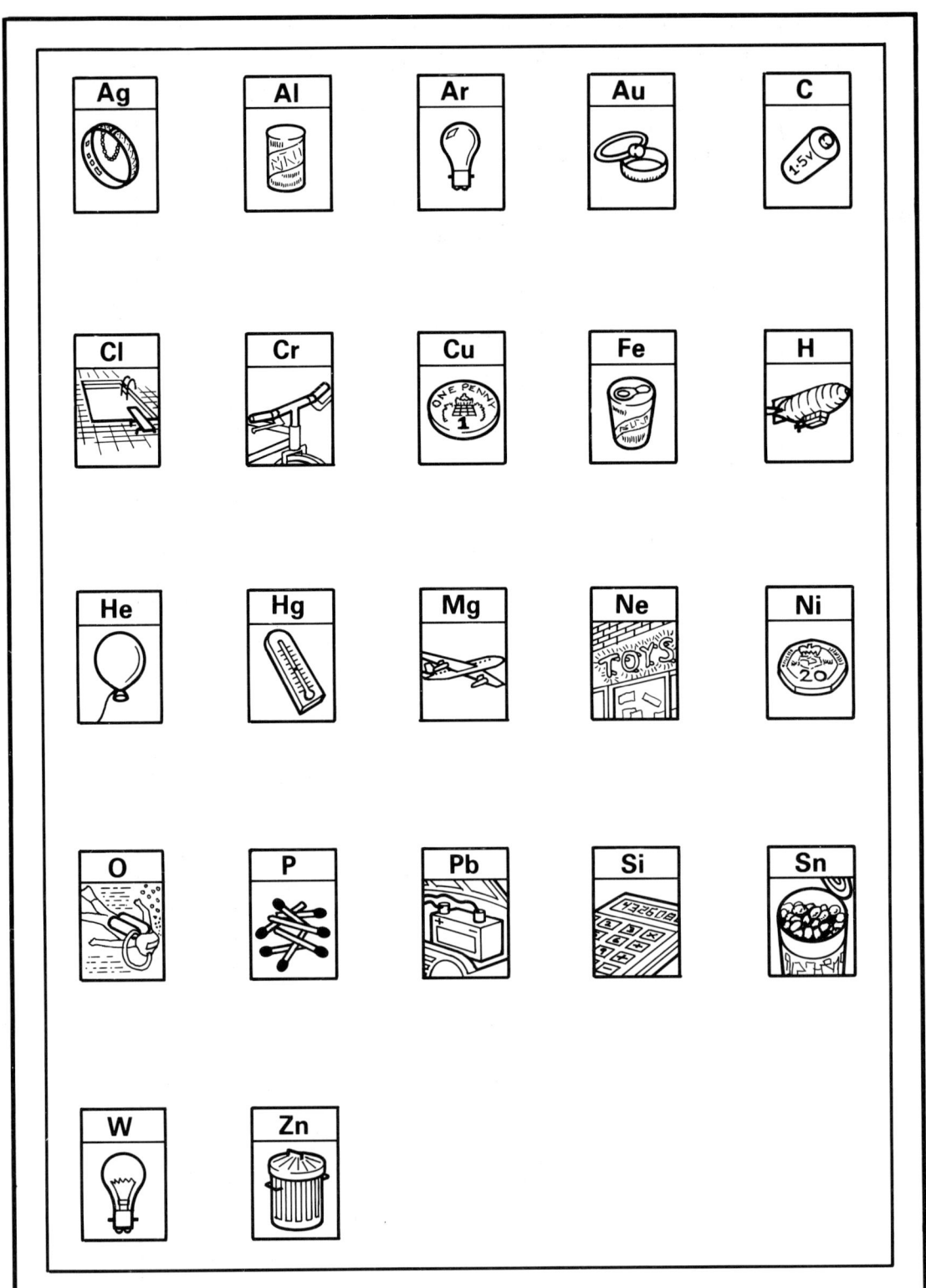

2 Each of the pictures supplied shows an important use of a chemical element. It is being used *as* the *element*. Of course, there are many other uses, where elements are joined together as compounds.

   a Cut out the picture, and stick it onto the correct position in the Periodic Table.

b For as many of the pictures as you can, write a sentence saying what the element is being used for, and why it is suitable. For example, for argon you might say "argon is used to fill light bulbs because it does not react with the hot filament".

Some of them are quite difficult, so don't expect to get a complete list.

© Borrows, Foster and Richardson 1991

Periodic Table

1	2											3	4	5	6	7	0
H 1 Hydrogen																	He 2 Helium
Li 3 Lithium	Be 4 Beryllium											B 5 Boron	C 6 Carbon	N 7 Nitrogen	O 8 Oxygen	F 9 Fluorine	Ne 10 Neon
Na 11 Sodium	Mg 12 Magnesium											Al 13 Aluminium	Si 14 Silicon	P 15 Phosphorus	S 16 Sulphur	Cl 17 Chlorine	Ar 18 Argon
K 19 Potassium	Ca 20 Calcium	Sc 21 Scandium	Ti 22 Titanium	V 23 Vanadium	Cr 24 Chromium	Mn 25 Manganese	Fe 26 Iron	Co 27 Cobalt	Ni 28 Nickel	Cu 29 Copper	Zn 30 Zinc	Ga 31 Gallium	Ge 32 Germanium	As 33 Arsenic	Se 34 Selenium	Br 35 Bromine	Kr 36 Krypton
Rb 37 Rubidium	Sr 38 Strontium	Y 39 Yttrium	Zr 40 Zirconium	Nb 41 Niobium	Mo 42 Molybdenum	Tc 43 Technetium	Ru 44 Ruthenium	Rh 45 Rhodium	Pd 46 Palladium	Ag 47 Silver	Cd 48 Cadmium	In 49 Indium	Sn 50 Tin	Sb 51 Antimony	Te 52 Tellurium	I 53 Iodine	Xe 54 Xenon
Cs 55 Caesium	Ba 56 Barium	La 57 Lanthanum	Hf 72 Hafnium	Ta 73 Tantalum	W 74 Tungsten	Re 75 Rhenium	Os 76 Osmium	Ir 77 Iridium	Pt 78 Platinum	Au 79 Gold	Hg 80 Mercury	Tl 81 Thallium	Pb 82 Lead	Bi 83 Bismuth	Po 84 Polonium	At 85 Astatine	Rn 86 Radon
Fr 87 Francium	Ra 88 Radium	Ac 89 Actinium															

© Borrows, Foster and Richardson 1991

turn

The periodic table

The Periodic Table is a useful way of sorting out the chemical elements. Elements with similar properties are arranged in families or *Groups*, which are the vertical columns.
As you move across the Periodic Table from left to right (across a *Period*) there is a gradual change in behaviour from metallic to non-metallic.

Element	Symbol	Atomic No.	Date of discovery	A B C D
Actinium	Ac	89	1899	
Aluminium	Al	13	1827	
Antimony	Sb	51	<1600	
Argon	Ar	18	1894	
Arsenic	As	33	1250	
Astatine	At	85	1940	
Barium	Ba	56	1808	
Beryllium	Be	4	1828	
Bismuth	Bi	83	1753	
Boron	B	5	1808	
Bromine	Br	35	1826	
Cadmium	Cd	48	1817	
Caesium	Cs	55	1860	
Calcium	Ca	20	1808	
Carbon	C	6	pre*	
Chlorine	Cl	17	1774	
Chromium	Cr	24	1797	
Cobalt	Co	27	1735	
Copper	Cu	29	pre*	
Fluorine	F	9	1886	
Francium	Fr	87	1939	
Gallium	Ga	31	1875	
Germanium	Ge	32	1886	
Gold	Au	79	pre*	
Hafnium	Hf	72	1923	
Helium	He	2	1895	
Hydrogen	H	1	1766	
Indium	In	49	1863	
Iodine	I	53	1811	
Iridium	Ir	77	1803	
Iron	Fe	26	pre*	
Krypton	Kr	36	1898	
Lanthanum	La	57	1839	
Lead	Pb	82	pre*	
Lithium	Li	3	1817	
Magnesium	Mg	12	1808	
Manganese	Mn	25	1774	
Mercury	Hg	80	pre*	

*=prehistoric

Element	Symbol	Atomic No.	Date of discovery	A B C D
Molybdenum	Mo	42	1782	
Neon	Ne	10	1898	
Nickel	Ni	28	1751	
Niobium	Nb	41	1801	
Nitrogen	N	7	1772	
Osmium	Os	76	1803	
Oxygen	O	8	1772	
Palladium	Pd	46	1803	
Phosphorus	P	15	1669	
Platinum	Pt	78	1735	
Polonium	Po	84	1898	
Potassium	K	19	1807	
Radium	Ra	88	1898	
Radon	Rn	86	1900	
Rhenium	Re	75	1925	
Rhodium	Rh	45	1803	
Rubidium	Rb	37	1861	
Ruthenium	Ru	44	1844	
Scandium	Sc	21	1876	
Selenium	Se	34	1817	
Silicon	Si	14	1811	
Silver	Ag	47	pre*	
Sodium	Na	11	1807	
Strontium	Sr	38	1808	
Sulphur	S	16	pre*	
Tantalum	Ta	73	1802	
Technetium	Tc	43	1937	
Tellurium	Te	52	1782	
Thallium	Tl	81	1861	
Tin	Sn	50	pre*	
Titanium	Ti	22	1791	
Tungsten	W	74	1783	
Vanadium	V	23	1801	
Xenon	Xe	54	1898	
Yttrium	Y	39	1794	
Zinc	Zn	30	pre*	
Zirconium	Zr	40	1824	

*=prehistoric

1 a This list shows when each of the elements was first discovered. Study it carefully, and in the final column write:
  A if it was discovered in the last 100 years (since 1890)
  B if it was discovered between 100 and 200 years ago (1791–1890)
  C if it was discovered between 200 and 300 years ago (1691–1790)
  D if it was known more than 300 years ago.

b Why do you think so many elements were discovered during the 19th century?
c Use coloured pens or pencils to shade in the squares of your Periodic Table, using a different colour for each of the categories A, B, C and D.
d What patterns do you notice? Which sorts of elements were known about a long time ago?

turn

© Borrows, Foster and Richardson 1991

WASTE PAPER

LOSS OF TRADITIONAL COUNTRYSIDE

For every tree which is chopped down, up to 6 more are planted in its place. The trouble is that these new trees tend to be special strains which are often alien to the area in which they are planted. What is more, they are planted at high density – equivalent to about 20 on an average sized modern suburban building plot. All this has resulted in the loss of traditional countryside and valuable wildlife habitats.

Excessive Waste

Just under ⅔ of our domestic waste is made up of paper and cardboard. Most of the 6 million tonnes of paper that we throw away in this country every year has to be buried in holes in the ground. This waste is a potential source of pollution when it degrades, releasing undesirable chemicals into the soil and air.

The energy needed to make recycled paper is 40% less than that needed to make new paper

HIGH ENERGY USAGE

The production of new paper from raw wood pulp consumes vast amounts of energy, the production of which in itself causes environmental pollution and adds to the Greenhouse Effect.

Chemical POLLUTION

Paper production involves a number of chemicals, the disposal of which can cause environmental problems. A big offender is chlorine gas used for bleaching wood pulp. Some organic chlorine waste products (dioxins) are very toxic and are difficult to break down. When they are released into the sea and rivers, they tend to build up causing local pollution.

---

1 a How do we get rid of most of our waste paper and cardboard at the present time?
  b What are the problems with this method of disposal?

2 From what is paper produced? Describe *two* of the problems which arise when new paper is made.

3 Recycling is a process that can be of benefit to the environment in several ways.
  a Name any other substances, other than paper, which can be recycled.
  b Describe how these items are collected.
  c Recycling must be worth doing. What do scientists have to think about before beginning a programme of recycling?

4 a Large supermarkets such as Tesco have been collecting waste paper for recycling for several years. What sort of items of waste do you think these firms collect?
  b Next time you go to a shop or supermarket, list all the products which claim to be made from recycled paper.
  c Plan a recycling programme for your school. List all the items of waste you would collect, and explain how you would encourage everyone at school to join in the programme.

© Borrows, Foster and Richardson 1991

Water to drink

EEEK! MY HAIRDO'S CHANGED TO GREEN

BOTTLE blondes were showering water chiefs with complaints yesterday after their hair turned **GREEN**.

Dozens of angry women protested about the bizarre effects of a breakdown at a water treatment plant.

The acidic water reacted with copper pipes to bring problems to 20,000 homes in North Cornwall.

Bleached blonde hair turned green. Bath water turned blue. Drinking the water caused ulcers and sore throats.

This story from the *Daily Mirror* shows some of the things that happened when 8% alum was accidentally added to the water supply in North Cornwall in July 1988. The acidic solution killed fish and attacked deposits in copper pipes. As a result, copper salts got into the water. These caused the dramatic changes in hair colour!

Water is not fit to drink if it contains too many bacteria. These microscopic living things breed in the water, and can make you sick if you drink it. Bacteria can be killed by carefully adding chlorine (swimming pool gas) to the water. Too little chlorine, and not all the bacteria will be killed. Too much, and the water will taste horrible and may make you sick. In large amounts chlorine is poisonous to people.

Most people in Britain get their water through pipes from a reservoir. The water must not be too acid, or it may dissolve the pipes. Lead pipes are especially dangerous because lead is quite poisonous. Copper pipes also cause problems—as the newspaper story shows. In some places the water is naturally acid, if it has collected over boggy peat moors. Lime may be added at the reservoir to get rid of the acid.

Water may stand for a long time in a reservoir before it is needed. Algae may grow in the water, forming a green slime. Sometimes copper sulphate is added to kill the algae. As the newspaper story shows, people can be poisoned by copper sulphate, so you must take care not to add too much.

Rivers often have tiny specks of clay floating in the water. These specks do not settle out easily, and so get carried into the reservoir, making it cloudy. People do not like getting cloudy water from their taps. Alum is often added to reservoirs to help the clay to settle out. Too much alum must not be used, as it will make the water acid.

Other chemicals may be added to the water. For example, fluoride is added to help make healthy teeth. Some people do not think this is a good idea, because too much fluoride is poisonous.

1 a Go through the information above. *Underline* the name of every chemical that is deliberately added to water. In a pen or pencil of a different colour, *underline* every reason for adding these chemicals to water. In a third colour, *underline* any problems the chemical can cause.

b Copy this table, and complete it with the help of your underlinings.

Name of chemical	Why added to water?	Problems

2 Go through the above information again. Put a ring round the name of everything that might be found naturally in the water. For each of the things you have put a ring round, decide if it is useful or a nuisance, and then copy this table and complete it.

Name	Useful or a nuisance?	Why?

3 Plan an investigation to see how much water your family uses altogether in a day. What would you need to measure? How could you measure it?

© *Borrows, Foster and Richardson 1991*

FAST FOOD

In Central America, over the last 20 years, the number of beef cattle has increased by two thirds. To provide grazing land for the cows, rain forest trees have been cleared and grasses have been planted for pasture. Where too many cows have grazed on the land, the grass has become replaced by weeds and heavy rain has eventually turned the forest into an eroded wasteland.

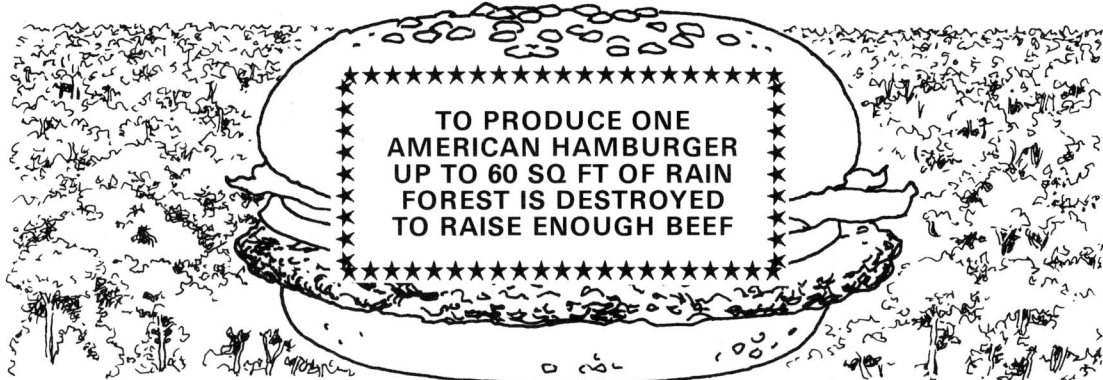

TO PRODUCE ONE AMERICAN HAMBURGER UP TO 60 SQ FT OF RAIN FOREST IS DESTROYED TO RAISE ENOUGH BEEF

If the present trend of destruction continues, an estimated 60 000 types of plants are thought to be in danger of extinction, or near extinction, by the middle of the 21st century. For every plant that becomes extinct, there are an estimated 20 dependent insects.

What do you get out of a Fast Food meal?

Many Fast Food burgers are made from beef that comes from European supplies. The chart shows the contents of some typical menu items.

Menu item	Energy (kilojoules)	Carbohydrate (grams)	Fat (grams)	Protein (grams)
Hamburger	1055	29.0	9.9	13.6
Cheeseburger	1255	29.1	14.2	15.8
Medium burger	1689	34.9	19.2	25.0
Large burger	2311	52.3	27.9	26.3
Regular Fries	1205	34.7	15.9	3.7
Large Fries	1612	46.4	21.3	4.9
Cola (regular)	400	25.5	0.0	0.0
Cola (large)	784	50.0	0.0	0.0
Chocolate Milkshake	1625	64.7	11.0	11.7

1 Why have large areas of rain forest trees been cleared?

2 What is meant by the word *extinction*? What important information is given in the sentence, *For every plant that becomes extinct there are an estimated 20 dependent insects*?

3 Shoab buys a Fast Food meal which includes a Big Burger, Large Fries, and a Large Cola. How much energy (in kilojoules) will this give him? Karen has a meal which includes a Cheeseburger, Large Fries and a Chocolate Milkshake. Will her meal provide more or less energy than Shoab's? What will be the difference (in kilojoules)?

4 a Draw bar charts to show the carbohydrate, fat and protein content of the four burgers.

b Which burger contains more fat than protein?

c Look at the chart again. Which burger contains a similar amount of carbohydrate to a regular portion of french fries?

5 Design a questionnaire to find out,
 – why people eat fast food
 – which type of fast food they prefer
 – how often they eat it.

© *Borrows, Foster and Richardson 1991*

Coming for a swim?

Britain's 7,000 mile coastline offers something for everyone: it may be a peaceful walk along the shoreline, a chance to breathe the bracing sea air or, for children the endless attraction of exploring the underwater life of numerous rock pools. What we don't expect however, is to stroll along a shoreline of dirty foam, dodging the litter and tar, even less do we expect to be confronted with lumps of human excrement while bathing. Unfortunately, this is what greets a large percentage of Britain's 62 million beachgoers even in the most popular resorts. As an island we have lost respect for the sea and assume it will absorb everything we throw into it. This includes sewage, both treated and untreated, along with a proportion of industrial and domestic waste, which, landing in the sea makes our beaches and bathing waters some of the most polluted in Europe with serious health and environmental implications.

Beaches conforming to EEC standards in 1986

Country	Beaches %
Holland	94
France	86
Ireland	85
Italy	81
Britain	44

Industries may be responsible for releasing heavy metals such as arsenic and mercury into rivers and the sea, together with massive amounts of phosphorus and nitrate.

Human excrement and sewage sludge may be responsible for releasing nitrates into the sea together with harmful bacteria and viruses.

Rubbish, directly released into the sea, may include beer cans, bottles and plastic bottles together with hospital waste and syringes.

Algae (a type of seaweed), grow very quickly in water containing high amounts of phosphates and nitrates. This can give rise to an algal blanket which covers the surface of the water and prevents oxygen reaching the fish. As a result these animals die. When the algae, themselves die, a gooey slime covers the water.

1 a Draw a bar chart to show the percentage of beaches conforming to EEC sewage standards in 1986.
  b Which country has the least number of beaches with a sewage problem?

2 a What is sewage?
  b Name a chemical which is released into the water when sewage is broken down.
  c What do scientists think this chemical does when it is in the water in large amounts?

3 Suggest ways in which
  a algae might be stopped from growing in such large numbers
  b the algae, already present, could be removed.

4 The article states that many of Britain's beaches are very unpleasant because of pollution.
If you were a scientist employed to make suggestions on how to clean up the beaches, what suggestions would you make? (A good idea would be to write your answer as a list.)

5 In the article above it is stated that both industrial and domestic waste are dumped in the sea.
Copy out the two tables. List the items of waste in each category. Suggest a reason why they are a problem.
An example is given to start you off.

Industrial waste

Item	Why a problem?
Nitrates	Algal slime

Domestic Waste

Item	Why a problem?
Beer can	Spoils beach

© Borrows, Foster and Richardson 1991

GENETICS BREAKTHROUGH POSES 'DESIGNER BABIES' DILEMMA

PARENTS of test-tube babies can choose the sex of their child, thanks to Robert Winston, professor of fertility studies at London University. But Winston, who revealed last week that he has found a *"totally reliable"* method of identifying whether a two-day-old embryo will be a boy or a girl, is confronting the ethical dilemmas raised by his breakthrough in genetic medicine.

Until now, the earliest that doctors could determine a child's sex was in the 15th or 16th week of pregnancy. By then, abortion is often the only realistic medical option offered to a woman if the foetus is likely to carry inherited disease.

Winston explained that two days after fertilisation the resulting embryo grows to eight cells. At this point one cell is extracted by a tiny probe inserted into the egg. Each cell in the embryo carries the full genetic blueprint of the future child, in the form of DNA molecules arranged into 23 pairs of chromosomes.

One chromosome pair carries the information that determines the sex: an XX chromosome identifies a cell as female, an XY as male.

In Winston's laboratory, the DNA in that single cell is replicated, allowing the scientists to determine whether they are male or female.

The process, which takes nine hours, kills the single cell, but the other seven continue to develop. Having discovered the embryo's sex, doctors then decide whether to implant it in the prospective mother's womb.

Winston insisted that the choice would not be for trivial reasons – *"for example, parents who have had three girls and would now like a boy"* – but only if there was a danger of genetically transmitted sex-linked diseases, such as muscular dystrophy and haemophilia, which affect only boys.

© *Amit Roy*. The Sunday Times
10th September 1989

1
  a Where are chromosomes found?
  b What is the total number of pairs of chromosomes found in a human cell?

2
  a What sex would a person be if they had XY in their chromosomes?
  b Look at the diagram on page 11 showing the crossing of a sperm with an egg. What chance is there that a couple will have a baby boy?

3
  a What name is given to the ball of cells formed after fertilisation?
  b How many cells make up this structure two days after fertilisation?
  c How many of these cells are needed to work out the sex carried by the chromosomes?
  d What must happen to the remaining cells if they are to develop into a baby?

4
  a A woman whose grandfather suffered from haemophilia, went to Professor Winston for this test. Why would she want to know the sex of her future baby at this early stage?
  b The article states that Professor Winston is confronting ethical dilemmas raised by this breakthrough in medicine. This means that many people are worried about whether or not what he is doing is morally right. What do you think are the major concerns of the people who are questioning this medical technique?

5 The other 22 chromosomes in the nucleus carry information that is passed on from one generation to the next. Either using your family as an example or the Royal Family, write down those characteristics which appear to have been passed on through the generations.

6 All human beings are different, that is, they show variations.
  a Find out the height of each of the pupils in your class.
  b Use a tally chart to group together pupils of the same height.
  c Draw a bar chart to show your findings.
  d Which height is the most common height in your class?

© Borrows, Foster and Richardson 1991

GENETICS

The sex of a baby is determined by instructions carried on the male sex cells from the father and the female sex cells from the mother. All cells in the human body, contain in their nucleus, 46 thread-like structures called chromosomes.

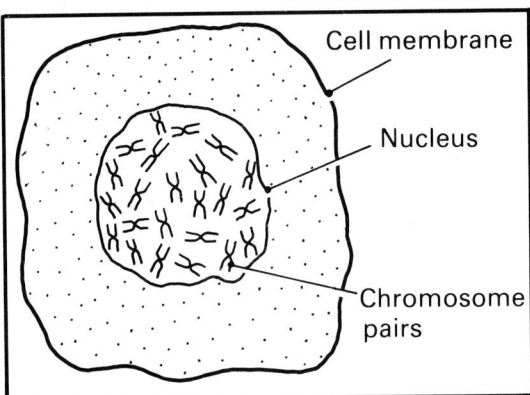

22 pairs of the chromosomes are identical, but the other pair of chromosomes may not look alike. These are called the sex chromosomes. Female cells have two sex chromosomes which *are* alike called **XX**. Male cells have two chromosomes which are *not* alike called **XY**.

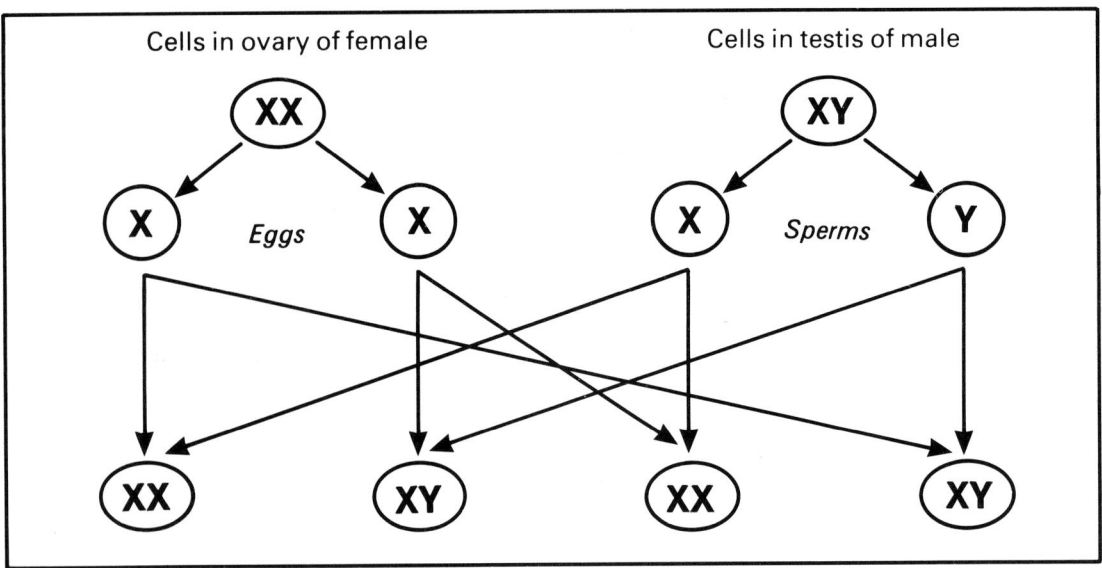

There are **four** possible ways of the egg and sperm joining together. The sex of the baby depends on which sperm fertilises the egg.

Parents	X	X
X	XX	XX
Y	XY	XY

© Borrows, Foster and Richardson 1991

"The refrigerator is the most powerful weapon we have in the fight against food poisoning, providing we use it properly."

Environmental Health Officer

Refrigerator do's and don'ts

DO'S

Use a fridge thermometer
Defrost the fridge regularly
Cover food
Place defrosted food at the bottom of the fridge

DON'TS

Place raw food beside cooked food
Leave the fridge door open
Put hot food straight into the fridge

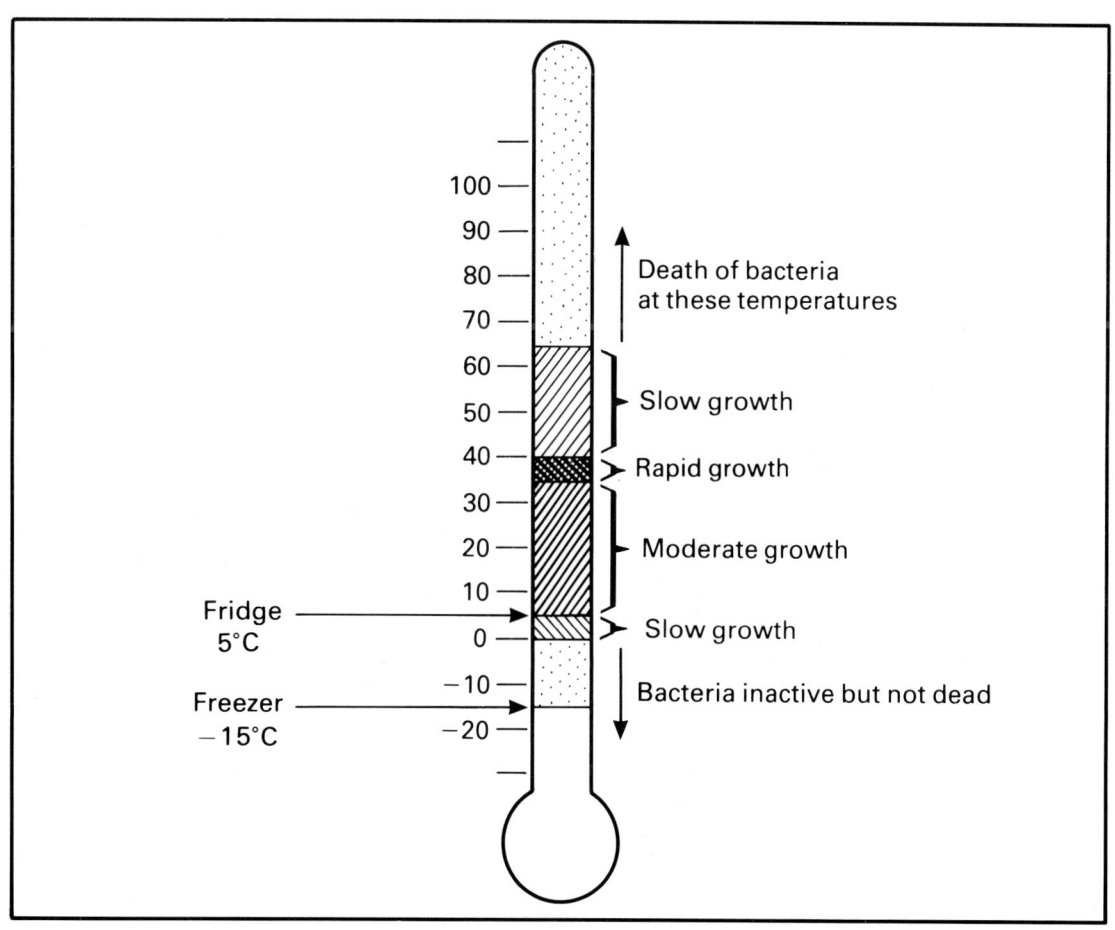

1 Use the information in the first paragraph on page 9 to estimate the number of food poisoning cases in 1978.

2 What is the ideal fridge temperature? Why is this temperature ideal?

3 Lucy goes shopping in her lunch hour for frozen beefburgers, a ready-cooked chicken and a jelly. She returns to her office for three hours before going home. She then places the beefburgers in the freezer, the chicken in the fridge and makes the jelly before placing it in the fridge to set quickly.

List the mistakes Lucy has made in handling this food.

4 Choose *two* refrigerator "do's" and *two* "don'ts". Find out why they are necessary actions if a fridge is to be a safe place for the storage of food.

5 Carry out a survey of family and friends to find out what they prefer about fresh food.

© Borrows, Foster and Richardson 1991

FOOD POISONING

In 1988 there were 30 000 cases of food poisoning officially recorded in Britain. This represents a three-fold increase within the past 10 years. The major outbreaks have occurred in centres of large-scale catering including hospitals, restaurants and schools. The figures, however may only reflect the tip of the iceberg as outbreaks in the home are rarely recorded due to the small numbers involved.

Microbes, or bacteria, are to be found everywhere. These organisms, however, are so small that they can only be seen using a microscope. Bacteria are often thought of as being germs, but only a few types of bacteria cause illness. Some bacteria are useful, such as those used to make yogurt. Nevertheless, it is important to prevent harmful bacteria from growing *on* or *in* food.

Food scientists have been working on different methods of food preservation for years. Food which is either canned or dried can be stored safely for months. This is because the bacteria are either killed or prevented from growing.

Many people prefer fresh food. This has a short shelf life and, therefore, should be stored in a refrigerator.

© *Borrows, Foster and Richardson 1991*

Drug abuse in sport

Sex hormones are released in males and females from puberty onwards. They control the development of the secondary sexual characteristics.

> ## OLYMPIC CHAMPION JOHNSON STRIPPED OF MEDAL IN DRUG SCHOCK
>
> **From JOHN JACKSON in Seoul**
>
> **SHAMED sprint star Ben Johnson – the fastest man on earth – was stripped of his Olympic gold medal early today after doctors found him guilty of using steroid drugs.**
>
> The Canadian athlete will automatically be banned for two years from international racing and forfeit the 100 metres world record he set in Seoul on Saturday.
>
> He will face a life ban if he uses drugs again.
>
> The International Olympic Committee voted unanimously for the ban after a urine sample taken after the race was found to contain traces of steroid.
>
> A top medical expert last night condemned the use of anabolic steroids which artificially create a superman effect.
>
> Professor Maurice Less from London's Guy's Hospital said: "Anabolic steroids build the muscles.
>
> "When little boys grow out of puberty their bodies start producing lots of anabolic steroids naturally to build up their bodies to turn them into men.
>
> "But when they take it from a bottle and inject it into themselves they are resorting to a dangerous and unnatural way of boosting that same process."

Doctors sometimes prescribe anabolic steroids to help recovery from serious illness but are very careful because the drug can have side effects.

Liver disease, acne, baldness, hardening of the arteries and cancer may be brought on by anabolic steroids. In women high doses of the drug may cause changes which are similar to the androgenic effects of the male sex hormones.

Male sex hormones		Female sex hormones
Anabolic effects	**Androgenic effects**	**Effects**
1 Growth of muscles	1 Voice deepens	1 Breasts develop
2 Growth of bone	2 Growth of body and face hair	2 Growth of pubic hair
	3 Testis and penis become larger	3 Widening of the hips

---

1 a When are anabolic steroids produced naturally by the body?
  b What is their effect?

2 How did the Olympic officials discover that Ben Johnson had been using drugs?

3 a In which sporting events has the illegal taking of steroid drugs become a problem?
  b Why do some sportsmen and women resort to taking drugs?

4 Describe all the risks a woman athlete is taking by using anabolic steroids.

5 Design a poster to be displayed in the changing rooms of a leisure centre, warning people of the dangers of using drugs.

© Borrows, Foster and Richardson 1991

Teeth and diet

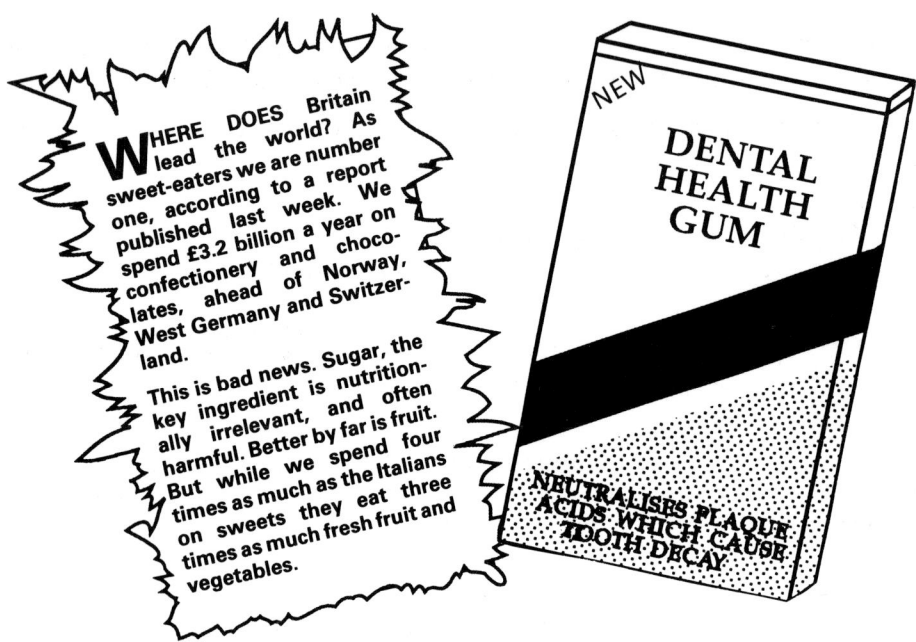

WHERE DOES Britain lead the world? As sweet-eaters we are number one, according to a report published last week. We spend £3.2 billion a year on confectionery and chocolates, ahead of Norway, West Germany and Switzerland.

This is bad news. Sugar, the key ingredient is nutritionally irrelevant, and often harmful. Better by far is fruit. But while we spend four times as much as the Italians on sweets they eat three times as much fresh fruit and vegetables.

An *ideal* balanced diet should contain protein, fat, carbohydrate, vitamins, minerals and fibre in the right amounts.

No food contains *every* nutrient in the right amount but some foods contain a lot more of one particular nutrient, for example, sugar in chocolate. Other foods may be rich in many nutrients, for example, bread.

Food	Protein	Fat	Carbo-hydrate	Fibre	Calcium	Vitamin A	B	C	D
Bread	✓		✓	✓			✓		
Softberry fruits				✓				✓	
Oranges				✓				✓	
Carrots				✓		✓			
Potatoes			✓	✓			✓	✓	
Cauliflower & Sprouts				✓				✓	

1 In the newspaper article it is stated that *sugar is nutritionally irrelevant and often harmful.*
The author is arguing that sugar is of little value in the diet and may cause problems. Write down why you think that eating too much chocolate or too many sweets may be harmful.

2 The author of the newspaper article suggests that the Italians eat a healthier diet than British people because they eat more fruit. Explain why this is healthier.

3 The Dental Health Gum is claiming to help prevent tooth decay.
  a Explain how the gum works.
  b List other ways in which tooth decay can be prevented.

4 Explain the part played by food in tooth decay.

5 Keep a diary for a week recording everytime you eat sweets, chocolate or sweet food which you know contain sugar.
Copy out the table below and tick in the correct box everytime you eat a sweet item.

Date	Hours in a day			
	0–6	7–12	13–18	19–24

At the end of the week look for any patterns you can see. Do you think you should try to change your eating habits?

© Borrows, Foster and Richardson 1991

Social drugs – alcohol

The Arabs gave us the word *Alcohol* thousands of years ago. They invented a process called fermentation, to make perfumes, but discovered alcohol by mistake.

The alcohol in all alcoholic drinks is the same but different drinks contain different amounts of alcohol.

½ pint beer   1 glass wine   1 measure whisky
All are equal in alcohol content

The information above is only a very rough guide as some beers may be very strong and others very low in alcohol. More detailed information, on the alcohol content of different drinks and the effects of alcohol, are given in the tables below.

Drink	Percentage alcohol by volume (%)
Whisky	40.00
White wine	12.00
Beer	5.50
Campari	23.60
Martini	14.70
Low alcohol beer	0.50
Low alcohol cider	0.60
Low alcohol wine	0.05

Units of alcohol	Blood alcohol levels (mg/100 ml)	Effect on a normal weight man*
less than 2	less than 30	Cheerfulness, increase in self-confidence
2	30	Increased risk of having an accident
3	50	Increased happiness, highly impaired judgement
5	80	Loss of driving licence
10	150	Slurred speech, loss of self-control
12	200	Inability to walk straight, loss of memory
18	400	Oblivion, maybe coma

* In general women develop higher blood alcohol levels and suffer greater ill effects than men, for a given number of drinks.

---

1 Draw a bar chart to show the percentage alcohol by volume of the drinks listed.

2 a How many pints of beer could a man drink before having an increased risk of an accident?
  b How many units of alcohol would make it likely that a man would lose his licence if he were breathalysed?
  c Can you suggest a reason why a woman might be in danger of losing her licence after drinking less than a man?

3 Fermentation is an important technological process. Find out what happens during fermentation.

4 Low alcohol drinks are now becoming more popular. Give *three* reasons why people are using these drinks.

5 It has been observed that the number of women convicted for drink driving offences has increased three times since 1974. What can you infer from this statement?

© Borrows, Foster and Richardson 1991

SUN DANGER

New cells are always being made by the body to replace those that wear out and die. In normal circumstances the rate at which these new cells are made is carefully controlled so that the right number are produced to replace the dead ones. Sometimes, however, cells can be triggered to multiply out of control, forming lumps. If the normal cells around the lumps are then invaded and destroyed, a malignant growth is formed which is known as a cancer.

WHAT'S THE OZONE LAYER?

Ozone is a gas in the atmosphere higher up than the air we breathe. It is important because it limits the amount of ultraviolet (UV) radiation from the sun that gets through to the earth.

When CFCs reach the upper atmosphere, they decompose to release the gas chlorine. The chlorine then reacts with the ozone to form oxygen. However, oxygen is unable to filter out the ultra-violet radiation.

In 1984 a hole was discovered in the ozone layer over the Antarctic which would allow more UV rays than normal to reach the earth. Medical scientists, believe that excessive exposure to UVb rays increases the risk of getting skin cancer.

WHAT IS A TAN?

In reality a suntan is no more than the skin's own protection against potentially damaging ultra-violet light.

On exposure to the sun's tanning UV (A) rays and burning UV (B) rays, the blood capillaries move closer to the surface of the skin, increase their permeability and create the redness all sunlovers are anxious to avoid.

The skin defends itself by producing melanin in its lower layers – a natural sunscreen which gradually moves to the surface of the skin, producing the golden colouring we all know as our summer tan.

Be safe in the sun

Despite recent publicity, there is evidence that people are still not aware of the very real risks of unprotected sunbathing.

The message is that skin cancer is preventable, and the sun can still be enjoyed without harmful side effects, if the right precautions are taken.

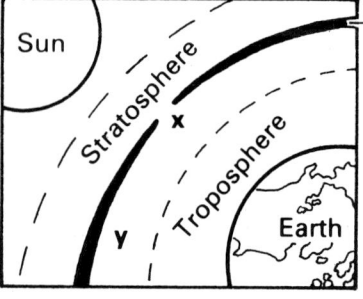

1 Copy the diagram.
  a Using lines and arrows, draw the pathway of UV radiation.
  b How is the amount of UV radiation reaching earth different at x and y?
  c What is x called?
  d Name a place on earth where scientists suspect that conditions at x already exist.
  e The troposphere contains the gases which we breathe. Name *one* of these gases.

2 a Name the *two* types of UV radiation from the sun.
  b How are these rays different in their effect on the skin?

3 a A sun tan provides the skin with protection against the sun. What substance, made in the skin, produces the sun tan?
  b A black skin provides a much better natural protection against the sun. Why do you think that this is the case?

4 All Sainsburys and Tesco own brand aerosols are CFC free and are clearly labelled. Explain why people are keen to buy these products.

5 The article *Be safe in the Sun* claims that skin cancer is preventable and that the sun can be enjoyed if the right precautions are taken.
Design a leaflet to inform people of the following:
  a What is skin cancer?
  b What precautions should be taken before, during and after sun bathing?

© Borrows, Foster and Richardson 1991

Social drugs – nicotine

WOMEN MUST GIVE UP SMOKING BEFORE THEY BECOME PREGNANT TO PROTECT THEIR BABIES, LEADING DOCTORS WARNED TODAY.

Mums-to-be who smoke during pregnancy risk damaging their unborn children from the minute they conceive, according to shocking new evidence.

Once you are pregnant it is TOO LATE. The damage has been done. You have already put your baby's life at risk.

Research published today shows that smoking damages the placenta – the unborn baby's lifeline.

The evidence will shock thousands of women who gave up immediately they discovered they were pregnant.

They still risk:
- GIVING birth to smaller babies who are more prone to complications.
- A 20 per cent higher chance of miscarriage.
- A HIGHER rate of stillbirth and death in the first week of life.
- A 25 per cent higher abruption rate after 26 weeks pregnancy. That's when the placenta breaks away and the baby dies.

Results clearly showed that, in order to prevent changes in the placenta, women **must stop smoking before conceiving**.

This research also shows for the first time WHY smoking is harmful to unborn babies.

The placenta works between the mother and baby, providing the baby with oxygen, food and antibodies, giving resistance to infection. It also enables waste to be removed from the baby.

THIS exchange is vital to the development of the growing baby.

The research team, funded by Action Research for the Crippled Child charity, showed that the membranes in the placenta, which separate the mother's and baby's bloodstreams, were thicker and the blood vessels smaller in smokers.

This impairs the transfer across the placenta and is harmful for the developing baby.

The placentae from women who had smoked at any stage in the pregnancy were quite different from those who had either never smoked at all or who had given up before conception.

"They feel they have killed their child."

Nicotine is the drug found in tobacco. It causes pulse rate and blood pressure to rise and, after prolonged use, may lead to the narrowing of blood vessels.

Smoke also contains tar and carbon monoxide, which with other substances may have harmful effects on the body.

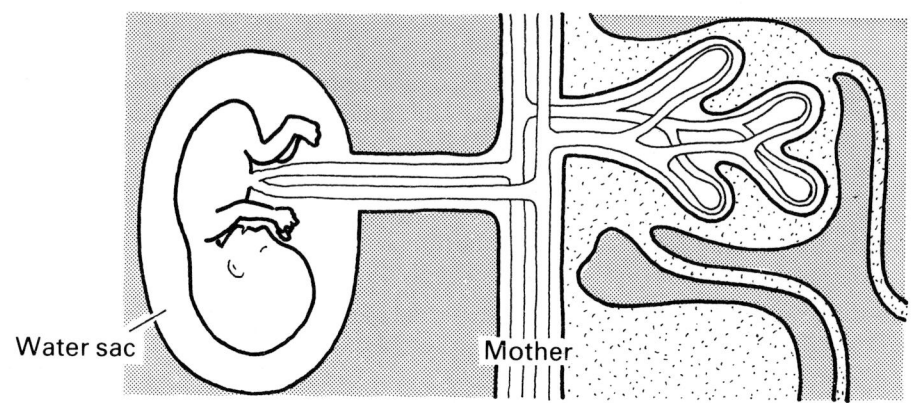

*Figure 1
Foetus (unborn baby) inside the mother's womb*

1 a Label the following on the diagram above; *baby*, a membrane between mother and baby called a *placenta, blood vessels* in the placenta.
   b Use arrows to show the direction in which the following substances move between mother and baby; *oxygen gas, food, antibodies, waste.*

2 All the evidence given in the article suggests that smoking during pregnancy affects the placenta. How do you think scientists gathered this evidence? *Remember* they would need to set up a fair test.

3 The author of this article is suggesting that women should give up smoking *before* becoming pregnant. Why is this important?

4 a Describe the main difference between the placenta of a smoking and a non-smoking woman.
   b Why do you think that these changes increase the risk of giving birth to a smaller baby which is more likely to suffer from complications?

© Borrows, Foster and Richardson 1991

On the street where you live

1 List the items of litter you can see in the cartoon. Give your answer in the form of a table and place each item either under the heading *biodegradable waste* or *non-biodegradable waste*.

2 Using either the street in which you live **or** your school playground, list all the kinds of pollution you have noticed (include sounds and smells).

3 a Why are toddlers more likely to suffer from toxicariasis than adults?
  b Describe the life cycle of the parasite which causes this disease.
  c What precautions can dog-owners take to prevent this disease?
  d What precautions can parents of young children take to prevent this disease?

4 Plan a local campaign against litter.
  a Look at the area in which you live (or go to school). What are the worst problems?
  b What might you do to help solve these problems?
  c Who would you need to involve in your campaign? How would you involve them?

5 Write an article for your local newspaper advertising your campaign against litter.

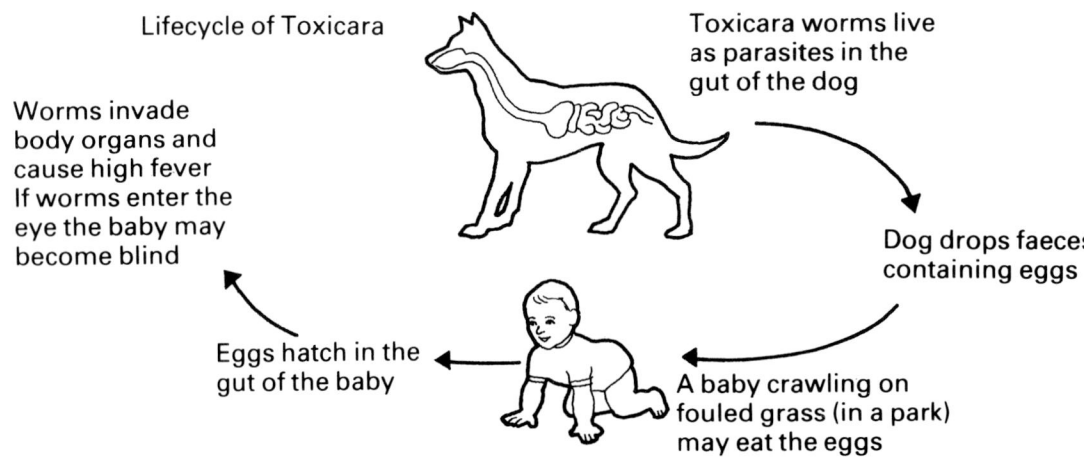

© Borrows, Foster and Richardson 1991

For most students, Key Stage 3 encompasses Levels of Attainment from 4 to 7, and we have aimed our questions at these levels. It is perhaps worth emphasising what a wide range of attainment this represents. The "average" pupil is expected to leave primary school at round about level 4: some undoubtedly will be working at level 5. But level 4 also is expected to correspond to GCSE grade G. Level 7, to be attained by a significant proportion of 14-year-olds is around the GCSE C/D boundary. In the past, teachers have perhaps tended to treat their lower secondary classes as fairly homogeneous, by no means stretching the more able, and ignoring the needs of the less able. The National Curriculum will cause a re-thinking of the level of work set to younger pupils.

We believe that the processes of science are fundamental: Attainment Target 1, the Exploration of Science, should interweave with all the other Attainment Targets. Accordingly, virtually all of the assignments have one or more questions relating to aspects of AT1. However, AT1 at the higher levels requires a considerable degree of collaborative work, and these assignments are mainly intended for (individual) homework, although some would be suitable for group work. Nevertheless, most assignments give opportunities for practising the component parts – making predictions, preparing written plans, etc – of this Attainment Target. We have tried to give a fairly comprehensive coverage to all of the other Attainment Targets, but in such a set of assignments there are inevitably gaps. For each assignment, we have identified a number of *Key Words* and *Phrases* which give the main subject matter of that assignment. This appears as the Index.

Peter Borrows
Stephen Foster
Barbara Richardson

In order to give teachers as much choice as possible, some of the assignments are quite lengthy, and may take more time than one conventional homework. When photocopying, teachers are free to blank out some of the questions, if they think there are too many, or if they cover work not yet done by the class, or perhaps if they are too difficult for the class. Generally, we have tried to incorporate an incline of difficulty, but sometimes the logic of the questions prevents the most difficult part being put last.

INTRODUCTION

The assignments in this book can be used for homeworks, extension works or to initiate topics in lower secondary classes. It is likely that they will be especially useful for homeworks where suitable resources are often not available. In particular, they can be used to consolidate ideas met in class or to give pupils the opportunity to read about Science.

Most of the assignments have three components, although with varying emphasis. There is some *Stimulus Material* – newspaper clippings, drawings of familiar objects, bottle labels, and so on. There is some *Reading Material*, sometimes summarising ideas that may have been met in class, sometimes introducing new ideas. Then there are the *Questions*. Sometimes these need brief one word or one sentence answers, but others require more extended writing such as planning an investigation, or carrying out and reporting on a survey.

In implementing the National Curriculum, many schools have focused on the Attainment Targets, and to some extent ignored the Programmes of Study. At Key Stage 3, the following statement appears as a part of the Programme of Study:

> **The application of science**: *pupils should be given opportunities to develop their awareness of the role and importance of science in everyday life, and, building on their earlier experience, their growing knowledge and understanding and their increasing maturity, to study how science is applied in a variety of contexts. They should consider the benefits and drawbacks of applying scientific and technological ideas to themselves, industry, the environment and the community. They should begin to make personal decisions and judgements based on their scientific knowledge of issues concerning personal health and well-being, safety and the care of the environment. Through this study, they should begin to understand how science shapes and influences the quality of their lives.*

It is at this part of the Programme of Study that we have aimed the *Stimulus Material*, and why we have called this collection of assignments "Everyday Science". It is too easy for teachers to say "Well, of course, I mention it in passing", and for it to pass by most children. The application of science needs to cut across all aspects of the teaching, and form an integral part of it. The stimulus material sets all these assignments firmly in the context of the application of science.

The *Reading Material* is partly intended to fill the textbook gap. It does include straightforward information, that teachers may well have mentioned in class. It sometimes includes a commentary on the stimulus material, or discusses further applications of science. It may repeat familiar scientific ideas in order to reinforce them.

The *Questions* are *not*, generally, intended as straightforward comprehension. Indeed, sometimes, they are only peripherally related to the stimulus material and/or reading material. In most cases, pupils will need to bring knowledge and laboratory experience with them. They are intended to reinforce work done in class, and are not independent of it. Generally, the sheets have been designed to be *not* consumable. This is not always true, however, as there are a number of DARTS (Directed Activities Related to Text) of the type suggested by Davies and Greene in the Schools Council publication *Reading for Learning in the Sciences*. These require the text to be marked in various ways with pens or pencils of different colours.

RADIOACTIVITY 2	*35*
DISASTERS	*36*
HOW THE PEAK DISTRICT WAS FORMED	*37*
THE ROCK OF THE PEAK DISTRICT	*38*
MOUNTAIN BIKES	*39*
THE GREATEST SPRINT RACE IN HISTORY	*40*
BATTERIES	*41*
SATELLITE TV	*42*
FREEZING TEMPERATURES	*43*
ELECTRICITY FOR FREE?	*44*
THE GREENHOUSE EFFECT	*45*
BIRD SCARER	*47*
LAMP-POSTS	*48*
SNAPPIT	*49*
THE EYE AND LASER SURGERY	*51*
VOYAGER 2	*52*
MOON AND EARTH	*53*
AIDS	*54*
KILLER IN THE CITY	*56*
LISTERIOSIS	*58*
SOCIAL DRUGS - *CAFFEINE*	*59*
INDEX	*60*

CONTENTS

INTRODUCTION	1
ON THE STREET WHERE YOU LIVE	3
SOCIAL DRUGS - *NICOTINE*	4
SUN DANGER	5
SOCIAL DRUGS - *ALCOHOL*	6
TEETH AND DIET	7
DRUG ABUSE IN SPORT	8
FOOD POISONING	9
GENETICS	11
COMING FOR A SWIM?	13
FAST FOOD	14
WATER TO DRINK	15
WASTE PAPER	16
THE PERIODIC TABLE	17
SOIL TEST KIT	20
LEMONADE BOTTLE	21
FIZZY DRINKS	22
PIPELINE	23
CRUMBLING CHURCH	24
ACID RAIN IN EPPING FOREST	26
RUSTING	27
MOLECULES IN THE AIR	29
ACIDS, ALKALIS AND INDICATORS ALL AROUND US	31
RADIATION TREATMENT	33
RADIOACTIVITY 1	34

ACKNOWLEDGEMENTS

The authors and publishers would like to thank the following for permission to reproduce copyright material:

Daily Mirror p.4, p.8, p.15, p.32 (right), p.33, p.36 (left)
Sainsbury's Living Today Series p.5 (left)
Holland and Barrett Suncare p.5 (centre)
Health Education News p.5 (right)
The Guardian p.7, p.32 (left), p.35, p.36 (centre), p.58
The Times p.12, p.45
Here's Health p.13
Tesco Free Leaflet p.16
Extra Newspapers p.26
Honda (U.K.) Limited p.29
The Independent p.36 (right)
The Observer p.40
The Sun p.42, p.43
Scope p.44
Today p.52
Daily Mail p.54
Evening Standard p.56

ASSIGNMENTS IN EVERYDAY SCIENCE

Thomas Nelson and Sons Ltd
Nelson House Mayfield Road
Walton-on-Thames Surrey
KT12 5PL UK

51 York Place
Edinburgh
EH1 3JD UK

Thomas Nelson (Hong Kong) Ltd
Toppan Building 10/F
22A Westlands Road
Quarry Bay Hong Kong

Thomas Nelson Australia
102 Dodds Street
South Melbourne
Victoria 3205 Australia

Nelson Canada
1120 Birchmount Road
Scarborough Ontario
M1K 5G4 Canada

© Peter Borrows, Stephen Foster, Barbara Richardson 1991

First published by Blackie and Son Ltd 1991
(under ISBN 0-216-92935-0)

This edition published by Thomas Nelson and Sons Ltd 1992

ISBN 0-17-4385803
NPN 9 8 7 6 5 4 3 2

All rights reserved. No paragraph of this publication may be reproduced, copied or transmitted save with written permission or in accordance with the provisions of the Copyright, Design and Patents Act 1988.

This publication is copyright but teachers are free to reproduce by any method, without fee or prior permission all pages with copyright lines, provided that the number of copies made does not exceed the amount required in their school or college. For copying these pages in any other circumstances (e.g. by an external resource centre), prior permission in writing must be obtained from the publishers.

Any person who does any unauthorised act in relation to this publication may be liable to criminal prosecution and civil claims for damages.

Printed in Great Britain

PETER BORROWS
STEPHEN FOSTER
BARBARA RICHARDSON

ARMTHORPE
COMPREHENSIVE
SCHOOL

ASSIGNMENTS IN EVERYDAY SCIENCE

KEY STAGE 3

Nelson Blackie